Rate Yourself as a Manager

Roger Fritz has 30 years' experience as a supervisor, manager, corporate executive, university president, and highly successful consultant to such companies as IBM, Pizza Hut, Catepillar, Brunswick, and Kitchens of Sara Lee. He is currently president of Organization Development Consultants, headquartered in suburban Chicago.

Prentice-Hall International (UK) Limited, *London*
Prentice-Hall of Australia Pty. Limited, *Sydney*
Prentice-Hall Canada Inc., *Toronto*
Prentice-Hall Hispanoamericana, S.A., *Mexico*
Prentice-Hall of India Private Limited, *New Delhi*
Prentice-Hall of Japan, Inc., *Tokyo*
Prentice-Hall of Southeast Asia Pte. Ltd., *Singapore*
Whitehall Books Limited, *Wellington, New Zealand*
Editora Prentice-Hall do Brasil Ltda., *Rio de Janeiro*

Roger Fritz

Rate Yourself as a Manager

A Practical, Workable Action Plan to Guide You to the Top!

A SPECTRUM BOOK

Prentice-Hall, Inc., Englewood Cliffs, New Jersey 07632

Library of Congress Cataloging in Publication Data

Fritz, Roger.
   Rate yourself as a manager.

   "A Spectrum Book."
   Includes index.
   1. Executives—Rating of.   I. Title
HD38.2.F75 1985   658.4'09   85-3539
ISBN 0-13-753237-7
ISBN 0-13-753229-6 (pbk.)

10 9 8 7 6 5 4 3 2 1

ISBN 0-13-753237-7

ISBN 0-13-753229-6 {PBK.}

Editorial/production supervision by Lori L. Baronian
Cover design by Hal Siegel
Manufacturing buyer: Frank Grieco

This book is available at a special discount when ordered in
bulk quantities. Contact Prentice-Hall, Inc., General
Publishing Division, Special Sales, Englewood Cliffs, N.J. 07632.

*To Kate, who has been the key to
realistic evaluations of my failures
and successes for 35 years.*

Contents

Managing Work 140

Managing Situations 197

Index 199

Preface

Everyone wants to be more successful. With success come respect, financial rewards, professional recognition, job security, personal satisfaction, and other worthwhile benefits. No one willingly accepts the alternates: dissatisfaction, frustration, and financial worries.

The purpose of this book is to help you become a successful manager.

Obviously, you would not be reading these words if the *interest* were not there. The objective of this book, then, is to help you convert that interest into a practical, workable *action plan* that will help you to be more successful.

Let me share with you three observations derived from my thirty years as a supervisor, manager, executive, and consultant to organizations in many fields. They are as follows:

1. The basic principles of management are the same, whether you are an entrepreneur of working with a multinational corpora-

tion; whether the organization is large or small; whether it is for-profit or not-for-profit; whether you are young or old, male or female; whether you live in the north, south, east or west; whether the economy is up or down; whether you are a neophyte or a veteran; whether you are low, middle, or upper management.

2. One's skill in management, like one's skill in golf or tennis, requires *constant practice.* Jack Nicklaus, possibly the greatest golfer ever to play the game, continues to work on the various elements of his game almost every day. Managers who grow too complacent or too lazy to continue practicing will eventually find their careers on a plateau—their futures at a dead end.

3. If managers *sincerely* analyze their own performance, genu-inely attempting to isolate their weaknesses rather than smugly looking for assurance that they are, in fact, performing well, and if they *take corrective action* to improve in any area of weakness they discover, their success will be virtually assured.

My aim in this book is to outline the key elements of good management, to help you realistically evaluate your performance in each of those areas, and to give you the guidelines you will need to follow when you find a need for self-improvement along the way. There are no magic formulas.

Jack Nicklaus is a champion not because his golf balls or clubs are any different from yours or mine but because he has learned to concentrate on the *basics* of the game, to *practice* those basics regularly, and to be *consistent* whenever he puts them to use. He is no more perfect than you or I. His ball may hook or slice off the tee. He may wind up in a sand trap. He may miss a two-foot putt. But Nicklaus is successful because he has made it a habit to *analyze* his mistakes, *determine* what caused them, and then *practice* diligently to see that he doesn't repeat them the next time.

Upward-oriented managers will approach their work in exactly the same way.

What one has in one's head is of little importance unless it is applied to the task at hand. To know *how* and to do *otherwise* is little better than never to have learned at all. When people err because they have been taught poorly, it usually is an easy matter to correct the situation simply by retraining them. But when those who have been trained properly ignore that training and err as a result, the situation may be far harder to correct.

This book is organized for quick reference, easy reading, and above all, immediate and productive *application* to your areas of individual concern. It will be most useful to you when used as a reference, to be consulted over and over as new situations occur throughout your career. Every success, every failure, every change in your personal situation provides a new reason—indeed, a new opportunity—to review your performance and to seek out critical areas in need of improvement.

My goal is to help you meet your goal by providing you with tools for successfully meeting this need.

ACKNOWLEDGMENTS

I am especially indebted to two people who have contributed in a variety of ways to this book. In both cases, the influence has extended over a long period of time.

George Odiorne first introduced me to the notion that only by focusing on objective evaluations of performance could organizations blend their long-term best interests together with those of the individuals who do the work. His help has continued in many ways but especially through his writings, which, I believe, are second to none in the practical application of sound management principles. He has, in a real sense, been a mentor for me for twenty years.

Bob Burns started me on the path of realizing that persistence pays off in helping organizations look for root causes of problems and not for superficial systems. He also taught me that there are no shortcuts in thinking through issues when many vested interests are involved. His always-sensitive and empathetic approach has enabled me to be much more aware of the fact that organizations can be changed from below. I also realize that an exclusive concentration at the top can mean that many golden opportunities for improvement may be lost by significant changes that can take place down in the ranks.

Although I will never be able to match George's wit and wisdom or Bob's clarity and persistence, my debt to both will never end.

What Is a Manager?

Yesterday's manager was characteristically authoritarian. Today, a successful manager is more likely to be a leader who stresses teamwork and cooperative achievement.

Today's managers are expected to think more deeply, understand more clearly, react more quickly, set a course more precisely, and stimulate others more positively than did their predecessors. Because of the problems and pressures of the moment, they often tend to feel that they *themselves* are being managed by a variety of outside influences.

EVOLUTION OF MANAGEMENT CONCEPTS AND SYSTEMS

Over the past fifty years, America has changed a great deal—educationally, politically, economically, and sociologically. The concepts involved in managing have changed accordingly, as reflected in Table 1-1.

Table 1-1. EVOLVING CONCEPTS & SYSTEMS OF MANAGEMENT & LEADERSHIP

Aspects	HISTORICAL		DEVELOPMENTAL		PROFESSIONAL
	Traditional Authority System	*Technical & Engineering System*	*Interpersonal Interaction System*	*Decision-Making System*	*Leadership Objectives System*
Image of Manager	A Take-Charge Type of Person	Scientific Manager	Interactor & Human Relator	Planner & Decision Maker	Professional Manager & Leader
World Of	Organization Chart, Policy Procedures	Principles & Fundamentals; Methods	Individual & Group Relations	Alternatives & Probabilities	Internal & External Forces
High Priests	Top Managers & Management Theorists	Industrial & Management Engineers	Psychologists, Sociologists Personnel	Economists & Organization Theorists	Entrepreneur Managers & Professionals
Language Approach	POIM: Plan, Organize, Initiate, Measure	Standard Operating Procedure	Relations Interrelations, Interdependency	Quantitative Decision	Plans of Action Rules Objectives & Rules
Organization Focus	Carry Out Policies & Orders	Primary Production Unit	Formal Informal Groups	Logic & Variables System	Balanced Corporation Trusteeship
Mood & Manner	Structured & Authoritarian	Austere & Imposed	Permissive & Clinical	Ordered & Programmed	Plans & Performance

Calculus & Concentration	Economic, Technical, Financial	Engineering & Operational, Technical	Motivational Behavioral Attitudinal	Economic Quantitative Structured	Results, Review, Improvement
Emphasis & Focus	Chain of Command, Channels	Work Flows & Efficiency Measures	Interactive Relations & Reactions	Logical-Rational Relationships	Autonomy with Accountability
Progress Review Procedure	A Trait-Based Administrative Club	A Form, Process, Procedure	An Interpersonal Interchange	A Technical Review	A Fact-Based Analytical Tool
At Worst It Can Be	Controlling, Directive Coercive	Bloodless, Mechanical, Instrumented	Evaluative, Pathological, Clinical	Abstract, Impersonal, Non-Human	Conforming, Controlling, Manipulative
At Best It Can Provide	Order, Direction, Progress	A Partial View of Management & Operations	Personal Interpersonal Behavioral	Logical Interaction Decision	Cooperation, Teamwork, Achievement

There is no perfect management system for all times and all situations. Concepts and systems have evolved over the past decades—and they continue to evolve today.

THE "LAWS" OF MANAGEMENT

Harold Geneen, the highly successful executive who guided International Telephone and Telegraph from a company of $700 million a year in sales to a multinational conglomerate with 350 divisions and more than $20 billion a year in sales, described his management philosophy in three "laws":

Law one: Highlight problems early and take action on them. Many managers park themselves in the middle of a problem and hope it will go away. Others ignore problems or pretend they don't exist. And there are even some people who settle right down in the middle of a problem and wallow in it, rather than fix it. Get problems out in the open, define them clearly with facts and objectives, and find a responsible person to assume the job of fixing them.

Law two: Facts must be facts. Never trust a person's opinion if his or her facts aren't solid. In this respect, most top managers would rate pretty high. There are damned few top managers who haven't been bitten at one time or another by an opinion that wasn't founded on fact. Making sure you are getting real facts and not biases, perceptions, or snow jobs isn't easy, yet it is a key building block of good executive management. If you're not able to trust a person's facts, you can't put much faith in his or her opinions.

Law three: All communication must be made face to face. You simply cannot operate a human organization successfully by sprinkling it with memos. You can't strike bargains, introduce change, or patch up fights by mail. Even when it takes time that I don't have, I know I'll get better results by using face-to-face contact in all goal-setting, performance-review, and feedback sessions. Meetings are for communication—and that means you can see as well as hear.

WHAT MUST BE MANAGED?

Dr. Robert K. Burns, cofounder of Science Research Associates and the founding director of the University of Chicago's Industrial Relations Center, offers a guideline regarding the *scope* of management. According to Dr. Burns, the tasks of managing can be divided into four parts.

Part one deals with managing *work* and can be called the *results* framework. Part two deals with managing *people*—the *personnel* framework. Together, they cover the management of an organization's economic and personnel requirements.

Part one
- Strategic Plans, Priorities, Follow-Up
- Managing by Objectives or Results

1. Define Role and Mission; define key areas; define priorities for results
   a. Clarification
   b. Consensus
   c. Commitment
2. Formulate Objectives
3. Determine Results to Be Accomplished in Priority Areas
   What?
   Where?
   When?
4. Review Progress of the Vital Signs
   Improve work
   Develop staff
5. Relate Managerial Objectives
   To budgeting
   To financial objectives

Part two
- Staffing and Strengthening the Organization
- Training, Performance, Development

1. Recruit and Select
   a. From inside the organization
   b. From outside the organization

2. Provide for Induction and On-the-Job Training
3. Establish Discipline Without Punishment
4. Determine Employees' Performance and Potential
   a. Assess
   b. Improve
   c. Develop
5. Provide for Managerial Reserves and Replacement
   a. Who is ready?
   b. Who is qualified?
   c. Who is available?

The other two parts of Dr. Burns's quartet cover the management of an organization's interpersonal and interactive requirements. Part three deals with managing *relations*—the *interpersonal* framework—and Part four with managing *situations*—the *interaction* framework.

Part three
- Communication
- Increasing Motivation, Cooperation, and Teamwork

1. Introduce the Climate-Setting Processes
   a. To develop trust
   b. To develop teamwork
2. Build Supportive Relationships
   a. Colleague-Helper vs. Critic-Judge
3. Use Effective Communication Techniques
   a. By questioning
   b. By listening
   c. By responding
4. Establish Basic Motivation
   a. Modify it
   b. Mobilize it
5. Coach and Counsel

Part four
- Handling Situations and Behaviors
- Problem Solving and Decision Making

1. Analyze and Handle Situations
   a. Study cause and reaction
   b. Analyze ends vs. means
2. Change Attitudes and Behaviors
   a. Groups
   b. Individuals
3. Use Constructive Confrontation
4. Reduce and Resolve Conflict
5. Share, State, and Solve Problems

HOW ORGANIZATIONS SUCCEED

Plato once observed that "the state is what it is because the people are what they are."

Managers who recognize the basic nature of their associates will accomplish more and hence be more valuable to their organizations. This entails an awareness of the following axioms:

1. Genuine improvement comes only from the active and voluntary cooperation of the people concerned.
2. People can do well only what they understand thoroughly.
3. When people understand, they tend to accept responsibility for solving operating problems.
4. If constructive action and implementation are to be achieved, organizational support is essential.
5. Productivity depends not on system-imposed or boss-imposed controls but on self-imposed goals adopted by individuals working together effectively.

FROM RESOURCES TO RESULTS

The overall objective of management is to use resources (inputs) to produce the desired results (outputs). *Inputs* include manpower, money, materials, and machines. *Outputs* include profitability, effectiveness, productivity, and results.

So-called *scientific* management techniques involve a bureaucratic system that involves:

1. Breaking a job down into its component parts
2. Creating a rigid, inflexible structure of organization
3. Establishing predictable relationships
4. Honoring supervisory personnel who adhere to organization and efficiency
5. Encouraging employees who will do what they are told

Organizations which choose *human relations* management techniques establish a social system within their business environments. This process involves stressing social relationships, pursuing group-centered activities, and honoring supervisory personnel who can foster the self-esteem of their subordinates.

Many modern companies have borrowed the best aspects from each of the two systems and formed what may be called an *organization development* management approach, which involves:

1. An organizational structure in which control is widely dispersed
2. Employing flexible, temporary systems that are designed for the needs of the moment
3. Stressing performance over personality
4. Stressing objectives over directives
5. Emphasizing job enrichment—giving jobs meaning
6. Selecting supervisory personnel for their team-building skills
7. Focusing on employees capable of self-direction and self-control

THE CONTINUUM OF MANAGEMENT STYLES

To help you even more as you explore your tendencies and style as a manager, consider the questions raised by Table 1-2.

Table 1-2. CONTINUUM OF MANAGERIAL STYLE

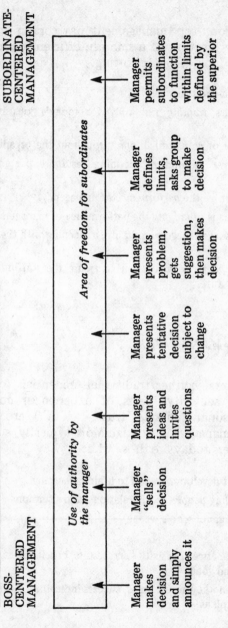

BOSS-CENTERED MANAGEMENT						SUBORDINATE-CENTERED MANAGEMENT
Use of authority by the manager				*Area of freedom for subordinates*		
Manager makes decision and simply announces it	Manager "sells" decision	Manager presents ideas and invites questions	Manager presents tentative decision subject to change	Manager presents problem, gets suggestion, then makes decision	Manager defines limits, asks group to make decision	Manager permits subordinates to function within limits defined by the superior

When (tasks, situations, time, personalities, etc.) is it appropriate to use each of these managerial styles?
Can a manager ever relinquish responsibility by delegating it to someone else?
Should the manager participate with subordinates once he/she has delegated authority or responsibility to them?
How important is it for the group to recognize what kind of leadership behavior the manager is using?
Can you tell how "democratic" a manager is by the number of decisions subordinates make?
What has a manager's value system to do with his/her managerial "style"?

HELP FROM THE TOP

Within any organization, top management has certain specific responsibilities for the creation of a smooth, efficient operation. At the very least, these include the following:

1. To *secure* and *hold* the best recruits.
2. To provide first-class *training* not only for today's jobs but for tomorrow's.
3. To improve the flow of *communications* throughout the organization.
4. To have an effective method of defining *results* expected from managers.
5. To continuously improve the *performance* of managers.
6. To have a reliable means of *judging* the performance of managers.
7. To *motivate* and *reward* managers equitably, in keeping with the results they have achieved.
8. To have a flexible *plan for succession* to assure the staffing of the organization in the future.

THE PROFESSIONAL MANAGER IS ...

Within these frameworks, neither traditional credentials (college degrees, certification, seniority, years of experience) nor less formal measures (personal contacts, trust, "clout") are really reliable in assessing a manager's potential. More typically, successful professional managers today are those who:

1. are committed to self-development and to lifelong learning
2. are effective in handling people, work, relations, and situations
3. look for what's wrong, not who's wrong
4. are self-motivated
5. know the difference between activities and results, efficiency and effectiveness, and tasks and goals
6. negotiate to determine key result areas, success indicators, measures of progress, and action plans

7. accurately analyze where we are, how much more we can do, and what we should drop
8. communicate accurately and regularly upward, downward, and across organizational lines
9. always ask *who* will do *what* by *when*
10. persevere through adversity
11. evaluate their own performances objectively
12. build upon strength: personal, subordinates', and the organization's

Becoming a Professional Manager

Professional managers must learn to do two things: help themselves and help their organizations.

To help themselves, they must:

1. Learn to manage themselves efficiently.
2. Continue to develop broad supervisory leadership abilities.
3. Seek new ideas and methods.

To help their organizations, they must:

1. Learn what authority is and how to use it.
2. Know the boss.
3. Know how to motivate.
4. Use performance-based tools that make supervision more than a "human relations" job.
5. Train their replacements.

Both of these tasks require careful study, and that must include study of:

1. The organization's structure.
2. Policies, goals, and objectives.
3. Group and intergroup relationships.
4. Responsibility and authority.
5. Means for self-improvement.
6. Growth and development opportunities.

Productive managers have learned a number of critical secrets that directly contribute to their success. These include:

- Having high standards of integrity.
- Being honest in their interpersonal relationships, and fair and equitable in the way they treat their subordinates.
- Knowing that loyalty can be developed only by a day-to-day, give-and-take approach.
- Viewing errors, mistakes, and failures as lessons.
- Having solid self-esteem, which transfers itself to the employees and directly affects their motivation.
- Using their own behavior to set the example for the group.
- Being objective in sorting out good and bad ideas.
- Possessing a keen sense of timing and knowing when to implement or discard a project.
- Knowing how to minimize bottlenecks caused by red tape.
- Perceiving and fulfilling the needs of subordinates through caring and interest.
- Being effective trainers and knowing that skillful training and effective management are inseparable.

CHARACTERISTICS OF SUCCESSFUL MANAGERS

Other characteristics commonly associated with successful managers are:

Impact: The ability to create a good first impression and to command attention and respect.

Communication skills: The ability to be persuasive, to make a clear presentation of the facts, and to be effective in written communications.

Judgment: The ability to reach a logical conclusion and sensibly handle the day-to-day affairs of a department.

Planning and organization: The ability to organize and control a function.

Initiative: The ability to originate action, rather than to wait for someone else to initiate it or delegate responsibility for doing so.

Sensitivity: The ability to recognize and respond to the needs of others.

Leadership: The ability to get ideas accepted, to guide a group, and to create a team atmosphere.

Creativity and problem solving: The ability to come up with imaginative, productive solutions to work-related problems.

CHARACTERISTICS OF
VERY SUCCESSFUL MANAGERS

Some people go beyond mere success and attain a status almost in a class by itself. While they demonstrate all of the characteristics that other managers do, they also possess two other qualities:

Compelling vision: An ever-present "consciousness" about the outcome they wish to achieve.

Concentration: The ability to *focus* their attention on reaching the desired outcome, neither fearing nor avoiding failure, but developing the capacity to take negative feedback without being destroyed by it.

FATAL FLAWS IN MANAGERS

Obviously, a manager has a great deal of flexibility in establishing or evolving a workable leadership style. Successful managers realize that times, tasks, circumstances, and personnel change; and that it often is wise to modify their management approach accordingly.

Some aspects of management, however, are nonnegotiable and are *always* to be avoided.

Do not fail to staff effectively.

Do not fail to think strategically.

Do not become insensitive to others and adopt an abrasive, intimidating, or bullying style.

Do not become cold, aloof, or arrogant.

Do not betray trust.

Do not become overly ambitious to the point of playing politics or ignoring the present job as you anticipate the next.

Do not overmanage to the point of being unable to delegate or build a team.

Do not become overdependent on some advocate or mentor.

Do not fail to learn to adapt to a boss with a different style of management.

2

Managing Yourself

To develop a sense of where you are and where you can go, it is important to have some feeling for the way in which you are perceived by others.

SEEING YOURSELF AS OTHERS SEE YOU

The following true-or-false quiz can help you to determine whether others see you as a participative manager or as an authoritarian one.

	True	False
1. I believe in accepting my subordinates' ideas, even when they differ from my own.	——	——
2. I believe that my instructions or procedures always should be followed as issued.	——	——

3. I usually try to get the support of people working for me before I proceed with an important policy change.   ___   ___

4. People in authority should present the *image* of authority in the way they dress, communicate, conduct themselves.   ___   ___

5. It is best to let your people implement your instructions the way they think best.   ___   ___

6. My subordinates need to be ruled with an iron fist. It gives them the direction and guidance they need.   ___   ___

7. I treat my subordinates as equals.   ___   ___

8. The suggestions I receive from subordinates are rarely very good, since these people do not have the range of experience necessary to see the picture as I do.   ___   ___

9. I rarely change the duties of people reporting to me without first talking it over with them.   ___   ___

10. Good managers give their subordinates complete, detailed instructions on how things should be done to get them done correctly.   ___   ___

11. I accept suggestions from people in my unit and very often use their ideas.   ___   ___

12. Consulting subordinates on important decisions wastes time, particularly when you want results.   ___   ___

13. One of the best ways to manage is to have regular staff meetings for soliciting ideas.   ___   ___

14. To cut down on lost time and frustration, I often do things myself, my way. Things get done faster, better, and more efficiently that way.   ___   ___

Having answered these questions as honestly as you can, add the number of odd-numbered statements that you have answered True to the number of even-numbered statements that you have answered False. If the total is 10 or more, you undoubtedly are looked upon as a participative manager. If your total is 5 or less, you're probably viewed as being an authoritarian.

TOWARD EFFECTIVE LEADERSHIP

Research has shown that individuals can improve their own leadership potential by taking one or a number of positive steps toward that objective. Such steps include:

1. Developing a work climate that encourages trust, candor, and open communications, including the willingness to share work-related information freely.

2. Adopting the belief that the best motivation is self-motivation and that—if the proper climate and leadership are provided—most employees will want to be productive and efficient.

3. Involving employees in problem solving and planning improvements whenever they are in a position to make a contribution.

4. Listening to employees and trying to see merit in their ideas.

5. Setting clear goals and helping employees to understand the organizational objectives.

6. Rearranging jobs to allow a greater degree of responsibility and self-direction.

7. Realizing that conflicts between the needs of individuals and those of the organization are inevitable but that these conflicts can and should be confronted openly—and resolved through the use of sound problem-solving strategies.

8. Using mistakes as an opportunity to faster learning, not as a means of placing blame.

9. Having high expectations of others, while providing them with support and encouragement to attain their objectives.

10. Providing recognition for superior performance.

MEASURING YOUR LEADERSHIP POTENTIAL

How would you respond to the following statements, proposed in the January 1983 issue of *Supervisory Management* magazine?

	True	False
1. Good leaders depend on their followers as much as they depend on themselves.	___	___
2. As a leader, I always tell a subordinate *why* when asking him to perform a task.	___	___
3. A good leader will achieve his/her objectives.	___	___
4. A key to good leadership is being consistent in how one leads.	___	___
5. If justified, I would recommend a subordinate for promotion to a position equal to or even above my own.	___	___

6. Some subordinates can participate in the decision-making process without threatening the leader's position.

    —— ——

7. Good leaders are born, not made.

    —— ——

8. I tend to treat my subordinates well as long as they do what I say.

    —— ——

9. As a group leader, I never entrust a vital project to anyone but myself.

    —— ——

10. If my group failed to achieve an objective because of a group member's failure, I would explain it as such to my superiors.

    —— ——

11. I consider myself indispensable to the company in my present position.

    —— ——

Those with high leadership potential would have marked the first six statements True and the last five False. Score yourself accordingly.

If your score is 9-11, you have excellent leadership potential and that ability is probably self-evident already. If your score was 6-8, you have good potential, but you need to fine-tune your thinking in the areas you answered incorrectly. If you scored 5 or below, you will have to adjust your attitude a great deal if you are to be successful as a manager and as a leader.

Remember, however, that individuals change over a span of time. Today's score does not necessarily reflect the way you will score next year—or five years from now. It is important to monitor yourself regularly, and to work at correcting any attitudinal weaknesses that such analyses may sometimes uncover.

BUILD YOUR STAMINA

One mark of the successful executive is the ability to work long hours under pressure, even after a discouraging setback. The secret is his or her physical and emotional stamina.

Stress is the main cause of fatigue. Fight it by letting off steam to a confidant. Repressed feelings of hostility consume a great deal of energy.

Uncertainty is debilitating. Know what goals are to be achieved.

Boredom is probably the most taxing stress of all. If you grow bored, find some work that is stimulating. Do things that promote relaxation. Keep a sense of humor, including the ability to laugh at yourself.

Recognize your personal limits and direct your energy toward positive goals.

Self-discipline is the best means of staying on the right track.

SUCCESS IS AN EQUATION

My longtime friend George Odiorne, who is one of our country's most highly respected management consultants, says that success (S) is the ratio of the amount of achievement (A) to the amount of expectation (E):

$$S = \frac{A}{E}$$

If you achieve a lot (A), but others expect more (E), you will not be rated as much of a success.

The secret, obviously, is to accomplish more than is expected. But what if the expectations become greater than that which you can achieve? Perhaps you have set unrealistic goals, promising more than you can deliver. Perhaps others have set their expectations too high because some important information has not been relayed to them.

Learn to communicate. Learn to set realistic goals. And learn to compromise, when necessary.

Does George Odiorne's formula help you?

What does it mean in regard to your relationship with subordinates? With your boss?

MAKING YOURSELF LOOK GOOD

In order to win a promotion, it's important to know what your superiors are looking for. Then, put your best foot forward.

Your boss will be watching for someone who:

1. Exhibits strong ability on his or her present job.
2. Is enthusiastic about his or her work.
3. Accepts the organization's goals.
4. Shows imagination and the ability to solve problems quickly.
5. Demonstrates flexibility and cooperation.
6. Has good interpersonal and communications skills.
7. Demonstrates the ability to get a job done on time and on budget.

GETTING—AND STAYING— ON THE RIGHT TRACK

Much depends not only on getting off on the right foot, suggests *Boardroom Reports*, but on staying on the right track.

If you are to be a good manager, you will:

1. Have the ability to "rise above the fray."
2. Perceive new, more creative arrangements of people and projects.
3. Cope with the resulting isolation.
4. Demonstrate self-control.
5. Show a sense of responsibility to others.
6. Share knowledge.
7. Be a mentor to subordinates.
8. Resist flattery.
9. Demonstrate patience.
10. Accept high-risk decisions.
11. Give clear direction.

QUALITIES OF HIGH-PRODUCTIVITY MANAGERS

Over a span of twenty-five years, the University of Michigan studied high-productivity managers. They found that such individuals:

- Place less direct emphasis on production as a goal.
- Are more employee-centered.
- Are good communicators and keep employees informed.
- Encourage employee participation in making decisions.
- Spend more time on supervision and less doing production work.
- Are less closely supervised by their own superiors.
- Have more confidence in their supervisory role.
- Know where they stand within the organization.

THE INGREDIENTS OF MANAGERIAL SUCCESS

Productivity is but one factor in achieving success as a manager. Also important are:

1. *Having a team concept.* One should care about the organization's progress and about the people working with one and for one—and show it.
2. *Working on one's weak points.* A person who can be honest with himself or herself can pretty well sum up his or her strengths and weaknesses on the job.
3. *Learning to delegate skillfully.* Perhaps one of the most difficult tasks for a manager is to learn to let go of an old job. Being willing to delegate is not enough; the delegation must be done thoughtfully and skillfully. Overdelegation is as damaging as underdelegation.
4. *Being realistic about inadequate subordinates.* A manager cannot let incompetent people drag him or her down. Once you lose confidence in a person and your efforts to help that person improve have failed, you must have the courage to make a change.
5. *Developing confidence.* Nobody is born with confidence; it must be developed. Confidence stems from successful accomplishment, and you can build on it day by day.
6. *Concentrating on preparation.* Good preparation breeds confidence. Combining preparation with enthusiasm will enable you to put your ideas across successfully.
7. *Being flexible in your thinking.* Don't think in black and white. Examine the other person's viewpoint carefully.
8. *Looking to the future.* Do not be satisfied with past successes. Each new job has its own standards for accomplishment.

9. *Using time wisely.* Concentrate on your most important responsibilities and schedule your time accordingly.

GUIDES TO BETTER EVALUATIONS

A strong sense of self-worth is important, but others often differ in their views of you—and *others* are the ones who do your evaluations.

You should get better evaluations *if:*

1. *You use a system of mutual goal-setting when performance standards are established.* General Electric Co. research has found that (a) performance improves most when specific goals are identified and (b) participation in the goal-setting procedure helps to produce favorable results. But don't try to help subordinates set up goals until you are absolutely sure of your own and those of your organization.

2. *You concentrate on performance and not on personality during the evaluative interview.* Keep in mind, however, that no one works in a vacuum, and that one's ability to perform well is always influenced by the total situation.

3. *You establish the proper relationship with each subordinate.* Employee development is a full-time consideration.

4. *You make use of praise as a supervisory tool.* When a subordinate does a good job, let him or her know that you appreciate it—and do so *at once*, not six months after the fact.

5. *You think of yourself as a developmental manager, especially when you set performance goals and correct on-the-job behavior.* Among the best supervisors are those whose authority stems from competence and knowledge, not from their job title.

6. *You do not discuss compensation during the evaluation interview.* Use the interview as a means of judging performance according to the objectives mutually agreed upon. Delay salary action until you have carefully considered:
   a. Current level of performance.
   b. Improvement or decline in performance since the last interview.
   c. How the worker's performance compares to that of others in the department.
   d. Market considerations.

Please notice that these considerations are equally appropriate whether you are the one being evaluated or the one doing the evaluation.

TENDENCIES OF GOAL-ORIENTED VERSUS TASK-ORIENTED PEOPLE

A goal-oriented person:

1. Seeks feedback and knowledge of results; wants evaluation of his or her own performance.
2. Considers money a standard of achievement rather than an incentive to work harder.
3. Seeks personal responsibility for work if goal achievement is possible.
4. Performs best on jobs where creativity can be applied.
5. Seeks goals with moderate risks.
6. Obtains achievement satisfaction from solving difficult problems.
7. Has high drive and physical energy directed toward goals.
8. Initiates actions; perceives suggestions as interference.
9. Adjusts level of aspiration to realities of success and failure.

A task-oriented person:

1. Avoids feedback and evaluation; seeks approval rather than performance evaluation.
2. Is directly influenced in job performance by money incentives; work varies accordingly.
3. Avoids personal responsibility, regardless of opportunities for success.
4. Prefers routine, nonimprovable jobs; obtains no satisfaction from creativity.
5. Seeks goals with either very low or very high risks.
6. Obtains satisfaction not from problem solving so much as from finishing a task.
7. May or may not have high drive; energies are not goal-oriented.
8. Follows others' directions; receptive to suggestions.

9. Maintains a consistently high or low level of aspiration regardless of success or failure.

Which kind of individual are you? Is your boss? Is each of your subordinates?

Warning! Not knowing your behavioral style may be hazardous to your career!

HOW DO YOU RATE
AS A SUCCESSFUL LEADER?

Here's another way to continue to look at yourself more objectively.

	Yes	No	Uncertain
1. Do I encourage participation by others?	___	___	_____
2. Do I have realistic goals?	___	___	_____
3. Do I continually question myself?	___	___	_____
4. Am I aware of group dynamics and loyalties?	___	___	_____
5. Do I become a part of the group before initiating innovations?	___	___	_____
6. Do I compete fairly?	___	___	_____
7. Do I have a high tolerance for frustration?	___	___	_____
8. Can I win without gloating?	___	___	_____
9. Can I lose without pouting?	___	___	_____
10. Do I control the impulse to "get even"?	___	___	_____

Choose the areas most need improvement and concentrate on them.

IMPROVEMENT PLAN WORKSHEET

Improvement Priorities

The areas in which I most need to improve are:

1.

2.

3.

The reason I want to make these improvements are:

1.

2.

3.

Action Steps

Concerning number one, I will take this action:

a.   by   __(date)__

b.   by _____

c.   by _____

The results I expect to achieve are:

a.   by   __(date)__

b.   by _____

c.   by _____

Remember: You have the ultimate responsibility to judge your own behavior, and you alone must take the responsibility for for change.

HOW TO KEEP YOUR CAREER IN NEUTRAL

If it is possible to prepare a list of *do's* that will help you toward a more successful career, it is equally possible to create list of *don't's*.

Those who believe their career success depends mostly on what others do or on "fate" are likely to be following these guidelines:

1. *Take it easy on the job.* If you work too hard, you may not have the energy to pursue your hobbies.

2. *Don't rock the boat.* Make each day just like the last. It's more restful.

3. *Complain a lot.* It lets people know that you're aware of the problems.

4. *Bad-mouth the boss.* Nobody is perfect. By pointing out the boss's shortcomings, loudly and often, perhaps you can help him or her to improve.

5. *Don't be loyal.* Think of yourself, first and foremost.

6. *Never admit your mistakes.* If you can't hide them, blame them on someone else.

7. *Take your personal problems to work.* You can work on them there in a more pressure-free environment.

8. *Don't take any initiative.* Why "give away" good ideas? Besides, you can't be blamed for something you didn't do.

9. *Gripe about your salary and working conditions.* If you don't let others know you're underpaid, you may never get a raise!

IDENTIFYING SUCCESSFUL FIRST-LINE SUPERVISORS

Here are four basic attributes of the successful supervisor:

1. *Desire for achievement.* Motivated mainly by achievement, successful supervisors accept reality. They "push" harder than their employees like, but they also "pull," which makes the pressure more acceptable. They establish the way to get things done and let everyone know what the goals are. They are not satisfied merely to delegate tasks and responsibilities; they may bypass their assistants to check details personally. They have self-confidence, but constantly worry about falling short of the objective. Achievement is their main concern, and they are respected (although not loved) by their employees for that. Some subordinates regard such supervisors as harsh taskmasters. They are!

2. *Attitude toward authority.* Successful supervisors support higher authority in working toward company goals. They accept the decisions of higher management. They regard higher authority as being more experienced, more knowledgeable, and more likely to recommend the most effective course of action—even when opinions differ.

26

3. *Ability to organize.* Successful supervisors *anticipate* most of the consequences of their decisions—the things that will happen next week or next month as a result of plans and decisions. They operate with confidence.

   Successful managers combine and arrange so that they know what is expected. Because they have anticipated the problems and systematically planned the work, their subordinates know that their supervisor is aware of what is going on, so they act accordingly.

4. *Attitude toward self.* Successful supervisors are often dissatisfied with their own performances. If they hadn't done this or that, or if they had done this or that better, the results would have been more satisfying. They are people with an itch to do better.

The employees must be convinced that their supervisor knows what they are doing and has their interests at heart. When a request is refused, a logical explanation is given. It may not be persuasive, but it is reasonable. Explanations are willingly made as to why rules are to be followed. Mutually acceptable answers will be found to work-related problems.

The successful supervisor insists that the job be done well and on time, and clearly is not softhearted about employees. He or she gets respect from employees by *influence*, not by formal authority.

How do you measure up in these four areas?

MY SELF-DESCRIPTION

With this background, this is how I would describe myself in terms of:

1. My desire for achievement:

   _____

   _____

2. My attitude toward authority:

   _____

   _____

27

3. My ability to organize:

_____

_____

4. My ability to gain the respect of others:

_____

_____

At this point, it would be a good idea to check your responses with at least one person who knows you *very* well—and preferably with three or four others. The purpose is to be sure that you are seeing yourself as realistically as possible *before* you begin to supervise others. Although it is never too late to change and view yourself more objectively, you will be far more effective in making judgments about others if your self-evaluations are accurate!

EMPLOYEE BEHAVIOR PATTERNS

In building an effective management team, we must not only consider our own leadership style but we must also evaluate the behavior patterns of others. We must try to use talents and experiences which supplement and complement each other.

Study these four employee behavior patterns in terms of motivation, and answer the questions that follow.

Supportive: Trusting. Responsive. Idealistic. Tries to do his or her best in assigned tasks. Sets high standards for self and staff. Highly receptive to others' ideas. Cooperates readily. Helpful. A natural team player.

Problems: Trust can become gullibility. Desire for excellence can extend to impracticality.

Keys to Motivation: Stress worthwhile causes. Appeal to idealism and sense of excellence. Ask for help. Show personal concern for his or her progress. Emphasize personal development goals. Be accessible. Give trust and recognition.

Controlling: Openly aggressive. A go-getter. Acts quickly. Expresses self-confidence. Persuasive. Very competitive. Takes charge. Wants little, if any, supervision. Tells *you* what needs to be done.

Problems: Initiative can become impulsiveness. Confidence can become arrogance.

Keys to Motivation: Appeal to competitive drive. Give maximum responsibility and authority. Avoid looking over his or her shoulder. Provide resources to achieve goals. Set boundaries, but appreciate initiative.

Holding/Conserving: Methodical. Precise. Analyzes alternatives thoroughly. Practical. Makes the most of existing resources. Often reserved and unenthusiastic. Does a predictable, efficient job.

Problems: Carefulness can become nit-picking. Methodical nature can become plodding. Analytical nature can lead to "analysis paralysis."

Keys to Motivation: Aim at methodical nature. Present ideas as low-risk. In launching new projects, accent links to existing areas. Show you are objective, fair, consistent. Set out details clearly. Be well organized. Systematically review how things are going.

Adaptable: Flexible. Enthusiastic. Tactful. Never seems to make enemies. Sensitive to what others want and modifies own approach accordingly. Seeks popularity and "the spotlight." Open to new ideas. Excites coworkers and subordinates to do the job at hand.

Problems: Flexibility becomes inconsistency. Tactfulness becomes overagreeableness.

Keys to Motivation: Capitalize on the project's social elements. Be informative. Provide helpful feedback. Keep the relationship friendly and relaxed. Keep manager's role central.

Analysis of contrasting styles

1. Which is your dominant style?
2. Your boss's?

3. Each of your subordinates'?
4. How can the various styles be blended?
5. How can they be used in forming project teams?
6. How should analysis of styles be related to the coaching process?

HOW TO CREATE FOLLOW-UP FILES

A follow-up system helps to keep us organized. It gets paper work off our desks, forces us to schedule tasks for specific dates, and prevents us from forgetting follow-ups and deadlines.

Before you set up a follow-up file, make up your mind that you're going to use it! It's not a place to stash paper work. It's not an aid to procrastination. It's a time-management tool to increase your effectiveness.

You are scheduling work to be done on a specific date.

Get into the habit of checking each day's follow-up file at a specific time—preferably the first thing in the morning.

Don't reschedule anything unless absolutely necessary.

If it's worth doing at all, it's worth doing at the scheduled time.

Keep Your Files Clean

If your files aren't properly organized and maintained, nobody will use them; and if they're not used, there's really no sense in having them at all.

Fat files waste time, not to mention space—and all of this adds up to money.

Here are six rules for a successful filing system:

1. *When in doubt, throw it out.* Don't file anything unless you feel you will have to refer to it in the future—and that not having it will cost the company.
2. *Use hanging files.* Don't jam manila folders into a filing cabinet by themselves. You want to be able to retrieve the items quickly.
3. *Don't use paper clips on materials to be filed.* Stapling papers together will keep them together and prevent the bottom of the file from becoming a collection of loose paper clips.

4. *Don't keep duplicate files.* You're only kidding yourself if you think it's more convenient for everyone in the office to keep their own copies. Chances are you'll never have to refer to 90 percent of the paper work anyway.

5. *Use colored tabs for alphabetical groupings or categories.*

6. *Before filing, decide how long you want the material to be retained.* Jot the month it is to be destroyed on the side of the page—and review and purge the files at least once a year.

HANDLING CORRESPONDENCE

There's a simple, three-step method for dispensing with paperwork: *Read. Decide. Do.*

Don't allow correspondence to accumulate. Set aside a time each day to go through your mail. If someone else opens your mail for you, make sure he or she separates it into Priority, Routine, and Junk mail. Have each category put in a separate folder, with the Priority folder on top.

Start with the Priority folder and work on it. If anyone else can handle the item, delegate it. If not, answer it on the spot. Use dictation equipment. Be brief. If the correspondence refers to an ongoing project, place it immediately in the appropriate project file, which should be within arm's reach in a desk drawer or credenza.

If some piece of correspondence cannot be answered until additional information is received, send it to the appropriate person with a request for the information. If the information already is on its way, place the letter in a follow-up file to be handled later.

Don't procrastinate by setting the correspondence aside. You'll forever be shuffling through piles of paperwork on your desk and forever dreading the task of "catching up" on the work you've postponed.

If you never get to the Routine or Junk mail, you won't have missed much. Give those folders back to your secretary and have them added to the next day's material—or ask the secretary to handle them for you.

Learn to work on Priority items first. These are the items which will bring 80 percent of your results. Resist the urge to shuffle through the mail, searching for quick and easy tasks. And don't waste time on interesting, but useless, literature. If some piece of sales literature looks as if it could produce a profit for your company, handle it right away or put it in a follow-up file. If it gives you an idea for your own promotion plans, put it in an Idea file to be sorted through once a week.

CLEAR THAT MESSY DESK

A cluttered office is not necessarily something to worry about. A publication called *Boardroom Reports* has said that a messy desk is a liability only if a good portion of your time is spent looking for papers.

Some executives can work efficiently and well at desks that are buried in paper. If you can find what you're looking for in three minutes or less, you really don't have a problem.

But if you *do* have a desk-top clutter that's impairing your productivity or efficiency, here's a way to solve it:

1. File all papers according to some kind of system. Any order, used consistently, is better than none at all. Try putting your papers in chronological order.

2. Process incoming papers as fast as possible to prevent a build-up. Delegate as much of this processing as possible.

3. Do not write notes on scraps of paper. It's one of the best ways to lose them. Write everything on paper of the same size. Use notebooks, which are easier to keep neat than file folders.

4. When traveling, carry a looseleaf notebook with needed information and room to accommodate more. Include recent phone messages, expense records, notes on upcoming projects, names of new business contacts.

PERSONAL INVENTORY
OF STRENGTHS AND WEAKNESSES

To make the best use of your time, an accurate self-assessment is vital. Rate yourself from 0 to 10 on each of the items listed below, with 0 meaning a characteristic of which you believe you have absolutely none; 5 meaning an average amount; and 10 meaning more than anyone you've ever known.

Score

1. I am well qualified for my job and the skills it involves. _____
2. I am very persuasive and usually get others to agree with me. _____
3. I get along well with others. _____
4. I am honest, not only with myself but with others. _____
5. I have great powers of concentration; very little distracts me. _____
6. I very quickly learn anything I put my mind to. _____
7. I am a natural leader, always in the center of groups and making things happen. _____
8. My health and stamina are excellent; I never feel too tired to do what I have to do. _____
9. I am self-disciplined and do what is required. _____
10. I am decisive, quick, and sure in my choices. _____
11. I am well organized. _____
12. I have a great deal of courage, am ready to forge ahead without letting fear keep me back. _____
13. I am creative, have new ideas, and am ready to hear the ideas of others. _____
14. I adjust rapidly to new situations and circumstances. _____
15. I have good judgment and often get hunches that I can follow to successful conclusions. _____
16. Other people recognize my leadership and are willing to follow. _____
17. I work well in a team situation and let others participate in the decision making. _____
18. I think I have a great potential for improving my abilities and my personality. _____
19. I am satisfied with my present goals at work and feel comfortable and optimistic about achieving them. _____
20. I have great energy, drive, and motivation to achieve my personal goals, and feel confident that I am using my energy wisely in meeting them. _____

HOW IS YOUR WORK AFFECTED?

Having inventoried your strengths and weaknesses, list four major personal strengths and four major personal weaknesses in Table 2-1.

Table 2-1. IMPROVEMENT PLAN

PERSONAL STRENGTH	WORK INFLUENCED BY THIS STRENGTH
1.	a. b. c. d.
2.	a. b. c. d.
3.	a. b. c. d.
4.	a. b. c. d.

PERSONAL WEAKNESS	WORK INFLUENCED BY THIS WEAKNESS	STEPS TO TAKE TO OVERCOME THIS WEAKNESS	IMPROVEMENT CHECK DATE
1.	a. b. c. d.	1. 2. 3.	
2.	a. b. c. d.	1. 2. 3.	
3.	a. b. c. d.	1. 2. 3.	
4.	a. b. c. d.	1. 2. 3.	

For each strength, list several parts of your work that benefit from this ability. For each weakness, list any parts of your job that suffer from it. Also, beside each weakness, note what you think you can do to improve the situation and set a date when you will reevaluate yourself to determine what progress has been made to overcome that weakness.

CHECK YOUR CONCENTRATION

In February 1983, *Supervisory Management* magazine presented a short quiz for checking one's ability to concentrate.

Read the statements below and indicate whether you Strongly Agree (SA), Agree (A), Disagree (D), or Strongly Disagree (SD).

1. I'm usually trying to work on more than two tasks at the same time. _____

2. I'm easily upset and bothered by arguments at home or work. _____

3. I work long hours and rarely have time for lunch, or even a break. _____

4. I'm spending less and less time on physical activities, hobbies, and other leisure pursuits. _____

5. I often work under distracting conditions, where noise, people, or poor lighting impede my accomplishments. _____

6. I can never get my tasks organized. _____

7. My job is no longer challenging; I'm bored and lack the motivation to get things done. _____

- 0-20: You've got your act together and know how to concentrate.
- 21-50: You're doing well and are pretty much in control.
- 51-85: You're wasting a lot of time with distractions and need to apply better techniques for concentrating.
- 86-100: You probably enjoy distractions and should begin to concentrate on why your score is incredibly high.

ARE YOU TIME-CONSCIOUS?

Unless you cultivate a respect for time and are constantly striving to use it wisely, you cannot expect to reach your ultimate in productivity. Ask yourself these questions:

1. Do you know how much one hour of your time is worth?
2. Do you have your day's schedule of activities firmly in mind when you reach your office?
3. Do you have a fairly accurate idea of what you ought to get done this week? This month? This quarter?
4. Have you delegated as much work as possible to subordinates?
5. Do you weigh the time requirements of various tasks before assigning them to others or undertaking them yourself?
6. Do you wade right into the high-priority, tough, and unpleasant jobs, rather than devote too much time to things that are easier or more pleasant?
7. Do you carry a notebook for jotting down ideas, information, etc., rather than rely on memory?
8. Do you use modern technology—calculators, dictation equipment, conference calls—to save time?
9. Is there a steady flow of clear communications between you and your people?
10. Do you constantly appraise—and police—your use of leisure time?
11. Have you developed routine ways of handling routine matters?
12. When things are going well, do you take advantage of the momentum by tackling other tough chores, or do you ease off?
13. Are you constantly looking for a more efficient way to get things done?
14. Do you have some fill-in jobs ready in case you discover some spare time (e.g., if a scheduled appointment is changed)?

Three or more "no's" to the questions above would indicate that it's time to change your ways.

WHAT'S YOUR TIME WORTH?

Based upon 244 eight-hour working days per year, Table 2-2 will show you how valuable your time really is.

Table 2-2.

IF YOU EARN	EVERY HOUR IS WORTH	EVERY MINUTE IS WORTH	OVER THE YEAR, AN HOUR A DAY IS WORTH
$ 8,000	$ 4.10	$.0683	$1,000
10,000	5.12	.0854	1,249
12,000	6.15	.1025	1,500
15,000	7.68	.1278	1,875
20,000	10.25	.1708	2,500
25,000	12.81	.2135	3,125
35,000	17.93	.2988	4,375
40,000	20.50	.3416	5,000
50,000	25.61	.4269	6,250

KEYS TO MANAGING YOUR TIME

A number of years ago, R. Alex MacKenzie wrote an article entitled "Toward a Personalized Time Management Strategy" for *Management Review* magazine. In it, he suggested the following techniques for improving one's use of time.

1. *Equal distribution.* No one has enough time, yet everyone has all there is. This is the great paradox of time: It is the one resource which is distributed equally to all.

2. *Time analysis.* A daily log of activities for at least one week, taken in 15-minute increments, is essential as a basis for effective time analysis. It should be repeated at least semi-annually to avoid reverting to poor time management practices.

3. *Anticipation.* Anticipatory action generally is more effective than remedial action. Expect the unexpected, and plan for it. Adopt Murphy's 3rd law: If anything can go wrong, it will.

4. *Planning.* Every hour spent in effective planning saves three to four in execution ... and gets better results. Both long-range and daily planning, formulated after business hours the previous day or early the same day, in consonance with near-term objectives and events, are essential to the effective utilization of a person's time.

5. *Flexibility.* Time should not be over- or under-scheduled. Flexibility may be necessary to accommodate forces beyond one's control.

6. *Objectives and priorities.* More results generally are achieved through purposeful pursuit of planned objectives than by chance. Time avail-

able should be allocated to tasks in ordered sequence of priority; otherwise, managers will tend to spend time in amounts inversely related to the importance of their tasks (Parkinson's 2nd law).

7. *Deadlines.* Imposing deadlines and exercising self-discipline in adhering to them aids managers in overcoming indecision, vacillation, and procrastination.

8. *Alternatives.* In any given situation, failure to generate viable alternative solutions will limit the likelihood of selecting the most effective course of action.

9. *Consolidation.* Similar tasks should be grouped within divisions of the workday to minimize interruptions and to economize the utilization of resources and the personal expenditure of effort.

10. *80/20 Rule.* A critical few efforts (around 20 percent) generally produce most of the results (around 80 percent). Effective managers concentrate their efforts on the "critical few" events, increasing the likelihood of their happening and therefore of achieving maximum results.

11. *Effectiveness.* Efficiency may be defined as doing any job right; effectiveness, as doing the right job right. Effort, however efficient, will tend to be ineffective if performed on the wrong tasks, at the wrong time, or with unintended consequences.

12. *Delegation/Decision level.* Authority for decision-making should be delegated to the lowest level possible, consistent with good judgment and available facts.

13. *Upward delegation.* Managers tend to encourage upward (reverse) delegation unwittingly by forcing their subordinates to be dependent upon them for answers. This results in the manager doing the work of a subordinate.

14. *Minimizing routine and avoiding detail.* Routine tasks of low value to overall objectives should be minimized, consolidated, delegated, or eliminated as much as possible. Managers should divorce themselves from unnecessary detail and selectively neglect all but essential information. This has been phrased "the need *not* to know."

15. *Limited response and selective neglect.* Response to problems and demands upon time should be limited to the real needs of the situation. Some problems, left alone, go away. By selectively ignoring these problems, much time and effort can be conserved for more useful pursuits.

16. *Exception management.* Only significant deviations of actual from planned performance should be reported to the responsible executive.

17. *Visibility.* To increase the certainty of achieving your objectives, keep the things you intend to do visible. You can't do what you can't remember.

18. *Brevity.* Economy of words conserves time while it promotes clarity and understanding.

19. *Tyranny of the urgent.* Managers live in constant tension between the urgent and the important. The urgent task demands instant action and drives out the important from our consciousness. Managers thus are tyrannized by the urgent and respond unwittingly to the endless pressures of the moment, but in so doing, they neglect the long-term consequences of the more important tasks left undone.

20. *Crisis management.* Managers often tend to treat every problem as if it were a crisis. This over-response causes anxiety, impairs judgment, results in hasty decisions, and wastes both time and effort.

21. *Interruption control.* Arrangement of and controls over activities should be designed to minimize the number, impact, and duration of interruptions.

STEPS TO BETTER TIME MANAGEMENT

Here are six steps toward gaining better control of your time:

1. *Gain time awareness.* The first step toward better time management is to undertake a critical analysis of how your time is spent.

2. *Identify "time robbers."* Which time-wasters stem from your individual style of management? Which are caused by others? Which can be eliminated or controlled?

3. *Set goals and list priorities.* Select five or six time-wasters that you want to correct, and prioritize them.

4. *Formulate action plans.* Prepare a list of tasks necessary to accomplish your goal of reducing lost time.

5. *Develop a time budget.* "Budget" your time, and use that as a personal planning tool for allocating time to specific tasks.

6. *Apply time-management principles.* Having determined how your time should be spent, set about the task of utilizing each minute to its fullest by
   a. Dividing large, difficult tasks into smaller, more manageable pieces.

b. Concentrating on priorities.
c. Tackling the tough jobs first.
d. Setting realistic deadlines.
e. Holding stand-up meetings, which don't last as long.
f. Consolidating similar tasks.
g. Putting your idle time to use.
h. Constantly monitoring your progress in eliminating wasted time.

The wise use of time requires the following:

1. *Self-confidence.* Set priorities and stick to them, especially when others confront you with conflicting demands.

2. *Concentration.* Time that is not interrupted is time that is productive.

3. *Flexibility.* Keep alert to changing circumstances and new methods. Don't get in a rut. Don't overlook faster, more efficient ways to work.

4. *A good memory, a good filing system—or both.* Know what needs to be done, by when, and what projects or reports will be due soon. Rely less on memory and more on a good filing system and checklists.

5. *A good disposition.* Unpleasantness almost always causes a disruption in work. Learn to control your own reactons so that you don't trigger unpleasantness in others.

6. *Honesty.* Be tactful but forthright. A direct answer or a truthful response is better than a vague or deceptive reply.

Poor use of time often means the following:

1. *Excessive tension.* Those who are constantly beset by tension will tire quickly, both physically and mentally, and fail to function effectively.

2. *Reliance on excuses.* You can't retrieve the past. Excuses or explanations for failure accomplish nothing—but waste time and energy.

3. *Indecisiveness.* Shifting from one task to another, or procrastinating on things that should be started right away, wastes time.

4. *Perfectionism.* If you get too wound up in doing things perfectly, you may never finish them.

5. *Negative emotions.* Hostility, frustration, and worry can sap your strength and keep you from accomplishing as much as you could otherwise. Procrastinators carry the burden of their undone work.

6. *Insecurity.* If you are unsure of your own abilities, you will waste time building up your ego and trying to impress others.

7. *"Workaholism."* Working every minute, at home, on vacation, and over a holiday, indicates a breakdown in the proper use of time-management principles.

WHAT TO DO AND WHAT NOT TO DO

To get the most out of your time, you should:

- Work on the big, important jobs and leave the smaller, less important jobs until later.
- Work on projects that are most likely to succeed, rather than on those that are sure to fail.
- Invest time and effort in areas where growth is both needed and possible.
- Beware of overemphasizing the parts of the job that you know best or like best.

You should *not*:

- Solve problems that aren't vital to your primary objectives.
- Work on problems that have no current solution.
- Spend time solving small problems that subordinates can handle.

BEWARE OF THE TOP FIFTEEN TIME-WASTERS

Five time-wasters that nearly always rank at or near the top of managers' lists are:

1. Telephone interruptions
2. Drop-in visitors
3. Meetings, both scheduled and unscheduled
4. Crises
5. Lack of objectives, priorities, and deadlines

These are closely followed by the next group of five:

6. Cluttered desk and personal disorganization
7. Ineffective delegation and involvement in routine detail
8. Attempting too much at once and unrealistic time estimates
9. Confused responsibility and authority
10. Inadequate, inaccurate, and delayed infomration.

Depending on the individuals, their particular leadership styles, and organization characteristics, five additional time-thieves often are mentioned.

11. Indecision and procrastination
12. Lack of unclear communication and instructions
13. Inability to say "no"
14. Lack of controls, standards, and progress reports
15. Fatigue and lack of self-discipline

Although the author has long since been forgotten, the adage holds true today: "When I misuse time, I have wasted the only resource I can never restore."

BAD TIME HABITS

For every act of poor performance there is a tailor-made excuse. When it comes to making poor use of one's time, the December 1981 issue of *Supervisory Management* magazine listed these five as the most common:

"I don't have time to plan." Planning is one of the most basic, yet essential, supervisory functions. Time spent on planning will *save* time in the long run. When planning, four questions need to be asked:

1. What are my objectives for the day?
2. What activities are required to accomplish those objectives?

3. What are my priorities?
4. How much time is required to do each task?

"I'm always available." While an open-door policy can help foster better communication, such a policy can reduce a supervisor's ability to control his or her time if it is carried to an extreme. Practice a modified open-door policy—and limit its use to specific times or circumstances.

"Let me do it." Supervisors sometimes willingly accept tasks and responsibilities that belong to others. Before a supervisor says, "Let me do it," he or she should immediately ask: "Is this really the best use of my time?"

"I'll drop everything." When faced with a crisis, some people overreact and drop what they are doing in order to deal with the demands of the moment. You must separate the urgent from the important.

"I have it right in front of me—somewhere." A supervisor should try to keep a clean, uncluttered desk and a useful filing system. Stacks of paper distract one's attention from working on one thing at a time.

HOW TO GET MORE DONE

Not all of the ways in which to "get more done" involve a great deal of fuss and bother. Here are six that require nothing but a slight degree of self-discipline:

1. Avoid unnecessary business lunches.
2. Keep your phone calls as short as possible. It helps to list all the things you want to cover before you place the call.
3. Handle correspondence immediately. If a short response is all that's needed, write it on the correspondence itself or handle it with a phone call.
4. Keep a notebook. Use it to jot down ideas and to list the things that have to be taken care of.

5. Analyze your activities. See where most of your time is being spent and then look for new ways to save time or cut down on labor in those areas.
6. Don't procrastinate. Establish deadlines for jobs and stick to them.

TEN MORE TIMESAVERS

"And Moses chose able men out of all Israel and made them heads over the people, captains of thousands, captains of hundreds, captains of fifties, and captains of tens. And they judged the people at all seasons: the hand cases they brought to Moses, but the small matters they judged themselves." (Exodus 18:25-26)

Moses, noted for his wisdom, was applying the first of the ten suggestions outlined below as a means of putting one's time to its best use.

1. Delegate responsibility.
2. Record everything you do, to the minute, for five days every six months.
3. Analyze your use of time, and eliminiate any unnecessary activities.
4. Set priorities.
5. Arrange for discretionary or creative time that you can call your own.
6. Avoid excessive management of past events which no longer can be altered.
7. Schedule and organize meetings for maximum efficiency.
8. Review your working habits at least once a month to be sure you're not drifting into time-wasting patterns.
9. Strive for quick resolutions to problems.
10. Try to complete each task you start so that you do not have to go back over it a second time.

HOW TO STOP PROCRASTINATING

Procrastination wastes time. Unfinished work always hangs over your head and reduces your effectiveness.

Procrastination is stress-producing. It frequently leads to last-minute rushes, to shoddy work, to missed deadlines, to lost sales, and to angry customers, bosses, or associates.

There is only one cause of procrastination: you. And there is only one cure: managing yourself. Convince yourself of the benefits of a "do it now" philosophy.

If the task is distasteful, tell yourself: "I'll do it now and get it out of the way." Force yourself. You will experience a sense of relief that will reinforce this "do it now" habit.

If the task is time-consuming, schedule large blocks of time well in advance. Mark them off on your planning calendar. Treat them as you would a meeting or an appointment. Work on the task at the appointed time(s), and it will soon be finished. The more time you block off at one sitting, the better; but even ten or fifteen minutes a day will eventually get the job done. If you wait until there is enough time to do it at a single session, you may wait forever.

CONSERVING TIME

Many people waste valuable, productive time by "revving up" for the day's work *after* they get to the office. A smart manager can reach peak efficiency much quicker if he or she:

1. Uses travel time to plan the day, draft letters, mull over new ideas, etc.
2. Takes home a letter or report that can be reviewed before leaving the house or can be read on the way to work.
3. Strikes up conversations with people on the way to work, helping to clear away "early-morning fogginess."
4. Leaves some unfinished (and interesting) work on subordinates' desks at the end of the day, encouraging them to plunge into it as soon as they arrive in the morning.
5. "Bribes" subordinates with a reward at the end of the day for completing all of their targeted work.

WAYS TO SAVE TIME ON THE TELEPHONE

The telephone is a valuable tool, properly used—but anyone who has had experience with teenagers can recite a frightening series of tales describing what can happen when the telephone is used improperly. You can get the most value out of your phone by:

1. Recording the best time of the day or week to reach the people you need to contact most frequently.

2. Trying to reach the boss just before 9:00 A.M. or just after 5:00 P.M. The secretary will probably be gone, and the boss will probably be there.

3. Asking as few questions as possible, which tends to shorten the conversation.

4. Installing touchtone phones. Dial telephones require at least four times as long to place a call.

5. Leaving a message, rather than holding—unless you have a lot of routine work you can be doing while you wait.

6. Jotting down the points you want to cover *before* you place your call.

7. Trying to get the information you need from someone else if the person you originally called isn't in. It saves a call-back.

8. Having your secretary screen incoming calls, handling as many of them as possible without you. Also, have the secretary return whatever calls you think he or she can handle without you.

9. Asking your secretary to note, when taking a message, the caller's phone number and the reason for the call.

10. Trying to settle the business *by phone*, then and there, whenever someone calls for an appointment. It gets the business out of the way, saves time later, and keeps your future calendar clear for other purposes.

DEALING WITH INTERRUPTIONS

Interruptions of any kind take time—sometimes at the least advantageous moments. An "open-door" policy doesn't mean you have to be available continuously. Discourage interruptions by having your employees accumulate their questions and holding brief stand-up meetings each day to air them. Hold those meetings outside your own office so you can control the length of the session by simply walking out once the questions have been answered.

When employees say, "Got a minute?" ask, "What is it?" If they simply need a yes or no, give them an answer; but if the question requires more time, schedule a meeting for later in the day or week.

Don't delay a priority project you're working on in order to work on some unscheduled activity introduced by an employee.

Schedule a "quiet hour" for each day, close your door, and make it obvious you don't want to be disturbed.

If possible, teach employees that a closed door means you don't wish to be interrupted.

To be effective, you must maintain control of your own time.

KEEP A DAILY TIME LOG

Daily time logs help you plan your day, help you remember important events, help you analyze how your time is being spent, and provide a reliable record of past events should it become desirable or necessary to have one.

A useful form is suggested in Table 2-3. My suggestion is that you record this information for five consecutive working days every six months. When listing your goals, describe them in terms of *results*, not *activities*. Record all significant acts during each fifteen-minute time period. Do NOT wait until noon or the end of the day and then attempt to recap the day's accomplishments, or much of the benefit will be lost.

At the end of the day, the following questions may help to increase the benefits of maintaining such a log:

1. Did setting daily goals and times for completion improve my effectiveness? Why? Why not?
2. What was the longest period of time without interruption?
3. In decending order of importance, which interruptions were most costly?
4. What can be done to control or eliminate them?
   a. Which telephone calls were unnecessary?
   b. Which telephone calls could have been shorter or more effective?
   c. Which visits were unnecessary?
   d. Which visits could have been shorter or more effective?

Table 2-3. DAILY TIME LOG (Example)

DATE _____

GOALS: (1) _____ (2) _____ (3) _____

(4) _____ (5) _____ (6) _____

Time	Action	Priority 1=Important & Urgent 2=Imp.—NOT Urgent 3=Urgent—NOT Imp. 4=Routine	Comment/Disposition/Results Delegate to _____. Train _____ to handle. Next time ask for recommendation. Next time say "No." Consolidate/Eliminate/Cut Time. Other.
8:00			
8:30			
9:00			
9:30			
10:00			

5. How much time was spent in meetings?
   a. How much was necessary?
   b. How could more have been accomplished in less time?

6. Did you tend to record activities—or results?

7. How many of your daily goals contributed directly to your long-range goals and objectives?

8. Did a "self-correcting" tendency appear as you recorded your actions?

9. What two or three steps could you take to improve your effectiveness?

TEN TIME TIPS FOR MEETINGS

To make meetings more productive and less wasteful of time, try following these ten suggestions:

1. Issue an agenda well in advance. Be sure to state the objective of the meeting. Include the starting time, time allocated to each item to be discussed, and anticipated stopping time.

2. When making up the agenda, put important items first to avoid rushing through them near the end of the meeting.

3. Invite as few people as possible.

4. Start on time, regardless. And don't summarize for any late arrivals.

5. Don't let people air their views unless it will help to fulfill the meeting's objectives.

6. At the end of the meeting, summarize the decision reached and the responsibilities assigned.

7. End the meeting when the objective has been reached.

8. Always evaluate the success of the meeting. Ask what could be improved the next time.

9. Keep minutes brief. Highlight the decisions reached and the action taken. Include deadlines. Pinpoint responsibilities.

10. Issue minutes promptly after each meeting while events are fresh in everyone's mind.

HELP SUBORDINATES MANAGE THEIR TIME

Helping subordinates to manage their time will enable them to accomplish more, but it will also help *you* eliminate bottlenecks, avoid delays and missed deadlines, and save time you otherwise might devote to excess supervision. Here are some suggestions:

1. Don't delegate everything to the same employee. Spread the work around and develop everyone's abilities.

2. Set deadlines on everything you delegate, but let the employee participate in setting those deadlines.

3. Accept the fact that employees need "quiet hours" as well. Don't interrupt them every five minutes. Let your questions or assignments accumulate so that you can interrupt only once.

4. Have employees write their own job procedures.

5. Provide training in time-management techniques, stressing those you have found to be particularly useful.

WHY INFORM?

Communication is the element that can make or break both personal and personnel relationships. Your progress as a manager can flounder for lack of this vital ingredient, even if you are generally effective in other areas of management.

Remember:

- Information and access to information are primary sources of power.
- People are most likely to do what is expected if they *know* what is expected.
- People usually can find ways to meet expectations and performance requirements *if* given feedback about results.
- Productivity can be increased when job incumbents receive clear and concise information about performance requirements and results.

YOUR COMMUNICATIONS EFFECTIVENESS

From time to time, we need to evaluate our communications effectiveness, both in transmitting and receiving ideas, feelings, and information.

In what types of situations are we especially successful? With whom? Why? What can we learn from these successes that will help us improve in other situations?

Managing is a series of transactions between individuals. The success of these transactions depends on how well those individuals understand each other. A manager is heavily dependent on what others do for him or her, and unless the concerned parties understand each other, it is difficult to attain the cooperation needed for accomplishment and progress. Things get done because people *cooperate* with one another to *achieve desired objectives* through meaningful and timely *understanding* (communications).

The most powerful communication is not what we say or what we write, but what we *do*. It is not what others are *told*, but what they *accept* and *believe*. People can do almost anything if they want to do it, are trained to do it, and understand the reason for doing it.

Using Table 2-4, rate the effectiveness of your communications, then consider how you would be rated by your boss, your suborindates, and your associates.

For each of the eighteen items given, list the name of the person within your organization with whom you communicate most effectively. Then, for each of the eighteen areas given, name the person with whom you could *most improve* your communications effectiveness. You might even encourage others to rate you as a communicator.

The payoff from this exercise will depend on your:

1. Recognizing your need to improve your communications effectiveness.
2. Identifying a few specific areas and subjects in which you need to improve and can improve.
3. Identifying the persons with whom you communicate effectively and the several with whom you need to do even better.
4. Planning your individual self-improvement program and committing yourself to putting it into effect.
5. Measuring the results and continuing your development as a communicator and manager.

In taking the quiz in Table 2-4, first grade yourself on *your* perception of your communications effectiveness, using a scale of 0-100, with 60 as a passing mark. Then, rate yourself as you believe your boss, your subordinates, and your associates would rate you.

Table 2-4. YOUR COMMUNICATIONS EFFECTIVENESS

How effective are you in communicating within your organization? Rate yourself (0 to 100; 60 passing) on each of the following 18 areas. (Definitions are on page 53.) Then enter for each of the 18 items how you think (a) your boss, (b) your suborindates, and (c) your associates would rate your communications.

YOUR COMMUNICATIONS
RATING BY:

	Rating of Yourself	Boss	Subordinates	Associates
1. Good news				
2. Bad news				
3. Plans				

Table 2-4. YOUR COMMUNICATIONS EFFECTIVENESS (continued)

YOUR COMMUNICATIONS
RATING BY:

	Rating of Yourself	*Boss*	*Subordinates*	*Associates*
4. Policies				
5. Changes				
6. Rumors				
7. What is expected				
8. How we are doing				
9. How we can improve				
10. Listening				
11. Directions				
12. Questions				
13. Complaints				
14. Suggestions				
15. Approachability				
16. Timing				
17. Objectivity				
18. Selling ideas				
TOTALS				

In a study of 1,000 managers, Professor Earl Brooks of Cornell University discovered that people taking the quiz in Table 2-4 gave themselves the following median ratings:

	Median percentages
Overall effectiveness as a communicator	81
Effectiveness in communicating:	
1. Good news	84
2. Bad news	71
3. Plans	70
4. Policies	67
5. Changes	76

		Median percentages
6.	Rumors	68
7.	What is expected	74
8.	How we are doing	76
9.	How we can improve	73
10.	Listening	83
11.	Directions	85
12.	Questions	79
13.	Complaints	74
14.	Suggestions	78
15.	Approachability	85
16.	Timing	74
17.	Objectivity	83
18.	Selling ideas	78

It is noteworthy that these self-ratings were lower than the overall median rating on thirteen of the eighteen items. Only on items 1, 10, 11, 15, and 17 did the respondents rate themselves higher than the overall median.

In general, the managers Professor Brooks studied believed that:

- Their bosses would rate them *higher* than they rated themselves.
- Their subordinates would rate them *lower* than they rated themselves.
- Their associates would rate them *about the same* as they rated themselves.

WHAT TO PASS ALONG

The previous quiz gives some indication of the types of communication with which a manager must deal on a routine basis. Using the same basic headings, let's explore each element in a little more detail.

1. *Good news.* Showing recognition of accomplishment, achievement, advancement, and other favorable situations.
2. *Bad news.* Reporting less progress than expected, missed promises, unacceptable quality, and similar disappointing results.
3. *Plans.* Explaining what is ahead, future and projected activities, both short-term and long-term.

4. *Policies.* Interpreting important guides to action and commitments concerning relationships, actions, and responsibilities.

5. *Changes.* Modifying assignments, schedules, priorities, dates, standards, and procedures.

6. *Rumors.* Handling unofficial and unconfirmed feelings, hopes, fears, and predictions.

7. *What is expected.* Letting others know what they are supposed to make happen. Setting objectives for quantity, quality, service, and cost. Imparting bases for judgment of performance.

8. *How we are doing.* Recognizing results currently and periodically in comparison to planned objectives.

9. *How we can improve.* Getting commitment for planned improvement in accomplishment, achievement, and innovation.

10. *Listening.* Hearing, giving attention to, and understanding others.

11. *Directions.* Instructing others on a day by day basis as to what is to be done, when, why, and how.

12. *Questions.* Asking and encouraging others to ask questions concerning uncertainties, interests, problems, and difficulties. Answering inquiries.

13. *Complaints.* Receiving and considering expressions of dissatisfaction, discontent, uneasiness, and resentment.

14. *Suggestions.* Receiving and showing consideration of ideas for improvement.

15. *Approachability.* Demonstrating availability when others need to communicate with you.

16. *Timing.* Imparting information at the appropriate time for desired results—neither too soon nor too late.

17. *Objectivity.* Reporting factually, without bias or prejudice and with due regard to personal feelings.

18. *Selling ideas.* Persuading and convincing others to accept suggestions and to take appropriate action.

QUESTIONS FOR COMMUNICATORS

The next time you must communicate with someone, *stop* and *think*, then *respond*. The following questions may help you to avoid dangerous and unrealistic reactions.

Ask yourself:

- Have I given this person a chance? Have I paid close attention to everything that was said—or did I "tune out" at a certain point?
- Do I assume that this person has nothing new to tell me?
- Is there an area of agreement that I have overlooked?
- Am I judging by what the person says—or by *how* it is said or what the person looks like?
- Am I reacting to any generalizations the person has made? Have I made any—without qualifying them?
- Have I looked for the middle ground in the issue? Or have I taken an "either-or" position?
- Have I taken too much for granted? Have I checked my assumptions against the facts?
- How do my inferences check out against the facts?
- Am I being objective? Or am I going on preconceived notions?

GETTING THE MESSAGE ACROSS

The *Dartnell Newsletter* has proposed ten suggestions for communicating *better*:

1. Share your information the first thing in the morning, when employees are fresh.
2. Get new information to employees quickly, and share all that you know promptly.
3. Focus whenever possible on what the topic means *personally* to the employees or, through them, to the customers.
4. Present not only the company's side of a controversial issue but other viewpoints as well, and let the employees draw their own conclusions.
5. Don't overkill a subject. Keep your presentation concise.
6. Call in someone else, such as a knowledgeable person or a higher-level manager, to present materials that you're not qualified to talk about or not really comfortable with.
7. Don't try to do the whole job yourself. Arrange for skip-level meetings.

8. After your presentation, follow up with further information or clarification.

9. If you're ill at ease when presenting information verbally, get some training.

10. Get out from behind the desk and talk to people occasionally. And ask them to talk with you from time to time about whatever is on *their* minds.

MANAGEMENT INCONSISTENCIES

Unfortunately, what we *say* is not always the same as what we *mean.* Some examples:

We say: "I plan." *We mean:* "Objectives are vague and contradictory."

We say: "I make decisions based on facts." *We mean:* "Emotions, opinions, and personalities come first."

We say: "I manage by objectives." *We mean:* "They may be *my* objectives, but the people who will do the work have not been involved."

We say: "I believe in job enrichment." *We mean:* "Pay is all I care about."

We say: "I use control systems to measure progress." *We mean:* "The things that we're measuring aren't important."

We say: "I do my job." *We mean:* "Much of my time is wasted on organizational politics and power plays."

THE LISTENING TECHNIQUES

Our objectives in listening to people are simple and basic.

1. We want people to talk freely and frankly.

2. We want people to discuss matters and problems that are important to them.

3. We want people to furnish as much information as they can.

4. As they talk them out, we want people to gain greater insight into and understanding of their problems.

5. We want people to try to see the causes and reasons for their problems, and we want them to figure out what can be done about those problems.

At the University of Chicago, Dr. Robert K. Burns compiled a list of "dos" and "don'ts" related to listening. He suggests that you *do* try to do the following:

- Show interest.
- Be understanding of the other person.
- Express empathy.
- Single out the problem, if there is one.
- Listen for causes to the problem.
- Help the speaker associate the problem with the cause.
- Encourage the speaker to develop competence and motivation to solve his or her own problems.
- Cultivate the ability to be silent when silence is needed.

What *not* to do is just as important as what you *do* do. Burns counsels against:

- Interrupting.
- Passing judgment too quickly or in advance.
- Giving advice when it's not requested.
- Jumping to conclusions.
- Letting the speaker's sentiments react too directly on your own.

The problems involving people and situations can be very complex, and there is an urgent need for managers to *listen* and to *understand* those problems. Often, we *think* we understand people and their difficulties when, in reality, we haven't even listened to them intently. We often think we understand a situation when, in fact, we have seen only a part of it—and experienced even less. We often think we understand the problems people face when, actually, we have only a surface knowledge of the facts and, in fact, are dealing merely with the symptoms and not the causes.

Listening is a key to *knowing* and *understanding.* One way to *know* more is to *listen* more and get more information. A person's judgments and decisions are only as good as the information on which they are based. One needs to discard the idea that one knows everything and has all the answers, because we never can know *all* about anything.

We need to approach people and their problems with greater humility, and to try to recognize the complexities involved. Discard the idea that other peoples' problems are simple, unimportant, and unworthy of your consideration. We need to listen with greater intensity, observe with greater acuity, and react with greater empathy. We need to synthesize what people say so that we can think and feel with more understanding.

You are listening poorly when:

- You are so busy framing your reply that your thinking gets in the way of your seeing and hearing.
- You feel dull and bored, unable to attend to each word.
- You are willing to dismiss the communicator as "unimportant" because he or she can be of no harm to you.

You are listening well when:

- You are able to repeat back, accurately and completely, what has been said to you.
- You notice the body language that goes with the verbal language.
- You aren't embarrassed to ask for a moment to think because you have been so busy listening that you haven't been able to frame your reply.
- You habitually find value in every person who seeks to communicate with you.

There are a variety of listening "techniques." Burns suggests five:

1. *Clarifying*
   Purpose: To get at additional facts.
              To help a person explore all sides of a problem.
   Examples: "Can you clarify that?"
              "Do you mean this . . ."
              "Is this the problem as you see it now?"

2. *Restatement*
   Purpose: To check meaning and interpretation with the other person.
              To show that you are listening and that you understand what is being said.

To encourage the speaker to analyze other aspects of the matter and discuss it with you.

Examples: "As I understand it then, your plan is . . ."

"This is what you have decided to do, and the reasons are . . ."

3. *Neutral*

Purpose: To convey that you are interested and listening.

To encourage the individual to continue talking.

Examples: "I see."

"That's very interesting."

"I understand."

4. *Reflective*

Purpose: To show that you understand how the person feels about what he or she is saying.

To help the individual evaluate and temper his or her feelings.

Examples: "You feel that . . ."

"It was a shocking thing, as you saw it."

"You felt you didn't get a fair shake."

5. *Summarizing*

Purpose: To bring all the discussion into focus.

To serve as a springboard for further discussion on a new aspect or problem.

Examples: "These are the key ideas you have expressed."

"If I understand how you feel about the situation . . ."

DEVELOP YOUR PLANNING SKILLS

To get an overview of your strengths and weaknesses as a planner, give yourself the following quiz. Score yourself 0-1 if the area is one of *definite weakness;* 2-4 if it's an area in which you consider yourself *rarely effective;* 5-6 if you feel you produce an *average performance;* 7-8 if you're *moderately effective;* and 9-10 if the topic area is one of your *definite strengths.*

1. Do I have a plan for spotting problems in the regular work-flow, then starting remedial action? _____

2. Have I set up checkpoints for monitoring work in progress? _____

3. Am I prepared to give answers regarding the work being done in my unit? _____

4. Do I have a grasp of possible problems involved in making changes in procedures and routines? _____

5. Do I work out—and stick to—deadlines? _____

6. Do I block out schedules, coordinating shared work responsibilities? _____

7. Do monthly reports for my unit indicate excessive overtime, failure to meet schedules, or serious complaints? _____

8. Does my unit have frequent unexplainable crises? _____

9. Have I trained subordinates so that work will continue even if I am absent or promoted? _____

10. Can I evaluate accurately the potential and limitations of people I supervise? _____

    TOTAL SCORE _____

If your total score is 90-100, you have definite strength in planning; 70-89, your planning skills are moderately effective; 50-69, your planning performance is average. If, however, your score is 20-49, it is evident that your planning rarely is effective; and 0-19, you need considerable training and effort to develop the planning skills necessary to be a successful manager.

STRESS ON THE JOB

Job stress can erode your efficiency, your productivity, and even your mental and physical health. You can get some indication of the degree of stress you are feeling on the job by giving yourself the following quiz.

If the statement that is given *never* applies to you, score a 1; if it *seldom* does, a 2; *sometimes*, 3; *often*, 4; or *always*, 5.

1. I'm not sure what's expected of me on the job. _____

2. Other's demands for my time are in conflict. _____

3. Commuting to and from work is a constant headache. _____

4. Management expects me to interrupt my work for new priorities. _____

5. I have a poor relationship with my boss. _____

6. I only receive feedback when my performance is unsatisfactory. _____

7. There is little chance for promotion in my organization. _____

8. Superiors make decisions or changes which affect me without my knowledge or involvement. _____

9. I have to work under crowded or noisy conditions. _____

10. I have too much to do and too little time to do it. _____

11. I feel uncomfortable with the political climate of the organization. _____

12. I do not have enough work to do. _____

13. The fear of failure is constantly on my mind. _____

14. I fear I am not qualified for my job. _____

15. I'm afraid someone else is getting ready to take over my job. _____

16. I feel pressures from home about my work hours. _____

17. I spend my time fighting fires, rather than working on a plan. _____

18. The organization is continually threatened by layoffs. _____

19. I don't have the opportunity to use my knowledge and skills on the job. _____

20. It seems I move from one deadline to another. _____

TOTAL SCORE _____

If your total score is under 50, you can relax and enjoy your work. The pressures are exceptionally few.

If your score is 50-60, you're experiencing normal on-the-job stress, and there's nothing to worry about. When changes must be made, make them selectively.

A score between 60-70 indicates a moderate amount of stress and indicates that some changes, made as soon as practical, ought to be considered as a means of reducing the pressure.

When a score ranges between 70 and 80, you are undergoing an abnormal amount of stress, and you should make some changes immediately. Between 80 and 90, stress has reached the danger point; and above, 90, you had better make some prompt, major changes *at once* or you will become the proverbial "basket case."

HOW TO HANDLE PRESSURE

Each individual has his or her own capacity for pressure and own mechanisms for coping with it. There are no "universal" rules for

helping a person deal with stress, but there are a few general guidelines that are worth consideration, as outlined in the August 1983
issue of *Reader's Digest* magazine:

1. *Don't be crushed if you fail.* If you indulge yourself that way, you will
   never put yourself in a pressure situation again . . . and you'll never
   grow. If you fail, go back over the situation from the moment things
   started to go wrong. Try to determine why. Figure it out. Then try
   again.

2. *Don't change your life radically when you're under sustained pressure
   or know you're about to be.* A pressure situation is not the time for
   making major changes. Wait until things calm down.

3. *You need the support and honest appraisal of your family and friends.*
   Embrace their help if they offer it. Ask for it if they don't.

4. *Keep it all in perspective.* You can't control everything around you,
   so don't try. No matter what kind of pressure you're under today,
   tomorrow will offer a new opportunity, a different perspective, a new
   cause for optimism.

5. *Do things that help you to relax.* Relaxing, stimulating, enjoyable
   things can do a great deal to take the edge off tension. The stressful
   situation may still exist, but you will be better able to handle it if you
   have released some of the pressure, even for a little while.

6. *Develop stamina.* Physical exercise is essential. Nutrition counts. So
   does a good night's sleep. But don't turn to alcohol or drugs as a means
   of dealing with pressure.

7. *Learn to* use *pressure.* Pressure brings everything together. Without that
   concentrated moment, it is not possible to hit your peak.

WHAT IS FAILURE?

Failure is a learning experience . . . a necessary pathway to success . . . an opportunity to try something new.

In *On Medical Education*, Thomas Huxley said: "There is
the greatest practical benefit in making a few failures early in life."

Failure often tends to make the individual lose perspective—
to feel that he or she alone has fallen short of success. Nothing
could be more foolish. No one throughout the pages of man's long
history has been free of failure.

In *For an Autograph*, James Russell Lowell pointed out: "Not failure, but low aim, is crime."

Obviously, Franklin Delano Roosevelt felt the same way when he said: "It is common sense to take a method and try it. If it fails, admit it frankly and try another. But above all, *Try something.*"

Somebody Has to Lose

The trouble is that we are conditioned to win. Losing often is traumatic. We make winning all-important. We can't accept failure.

Losing can deepen understanding. Increase our appreciation for others. Develop greater empathy and sympathy. Produce authentic humility. Soften character. Mature the ego.

Winning, on the other hand, is not free of pitfalls. It can encourage arrogance. It can nurture impatience with others. It may stimulate contempt for the less fortunate. It can harden character—and inflate the ego.

Reality is winning *and* losing. Prepare for reality—and learn from both.

How to Create Failure

As difficult as it may be to believe, some people unnecessarily *create* failure situations for themselves. Such situations are psychological setups that feed the individual's insecurity and professional doubt, and they are breeding grounds for stress.

Some examples:

- You habitually accept more work than you possibly can get done.
- You create, and then don't meet, unrealistic personal deadlines.
- You must be Number One in everything that you do.
- You acknowledge only what you do wrong and ignore what you do right.
- Without any evidence to that effect, you believe that you have disappointed someone important to you.
- You set, then fail to meet, perfectionist standards.
- You feel cheated and insecure every time someone else gets ahead.
- You have developed the habit of procrastinating.

Coping with Failure

Many people who seek success have been conditioned to stop the pursuit *short of their goal* for one overpowering reason—fear of failing. As you change your attitude toward failure and rejection, performance can improve. To do so, follow these suggestions:

1. Accept the challenge to *know yourself better* so that you can develop your own potential. Determine which responsibilities or activities you tend to avoid.

2. Watch how you react to negatives. Ask: "Which is more important to me, to achieve something significant or to avoid failure?" Resolve to handle the possibility of failure as you pursue significant performance.

3. Determine how you can eliminate obstacles that smother growth. Too often, we accept obstacles that we could have removed. Once the obstacle is removed, the path of achievement and success becomes more clear.

4. Understand that failure and success are both a part of the process of achieving. One must know how to feel successful, even when he or she is falling short of success much of the time.

5. Failure alone shouldn't really bother you. It is the rejection often associated with failure that concerns us. Learn to cope with rejection. People often are successful largely because of their ability to handle failure.

Babe Ruth's strikeout record was among the highest in baseball history. He is not remembered for that but for his home-run success. Fans of Ruth know, however, that he reacted identically to the cheers that greeted a game-winning home run and the jeers that greeted a game-losing strikeout. He'd doff his cap and wave to the crowd! Babe Ruth conditioned himself to react successfully whether he was succeeding or failing. Home run or strikeout, his reaction was the same.

HOW TO HANDLE REJECTION

As a practice exercise in handling rejection, give yourself this little Yes-or-No quiz formulated by *Success* magazine in October 1982.

1. If someone says "no" to you, criticizes or becomes angry at you, do you usually feel rejected? _____

2. When rejected, do you generally feel that it's because of something you are or something that you have done wrong? _____

3. Whether it was the clothes you wore or the resume you sent, or perhaps a remark someone made about you, do you make sure to find out the specific reason you were rejected? _____

4. If you are rejected, does it take you longer than 20 minutes to decide to do something about it, rather than withdrawing? _____

5. When you decide to do something about a rejection, do you have a system or plan to figure out the best way to overcome the rejection? _____

6. When you probe into the possible reason for a rejection, do you ever think: "I actually set myself up for this?" _____

7. Do you give yourself permission, now and then, to fail? _____

8. Is your feeling of rejection—or the intensity of it—partly due to the fact that you're currently more vulnerable than usual or under a greater amount of pressure? _____

9. Is it difficult for you to reject others, even in the most humane way possible, when they deserve it? _____

10. Does simple rejection seem to mean more than that to you—something out of proportion to the situation? _____

The proper responses should have been:

1. No. Anger, criticism and refusal are not the same as rejection. People who love us frequently become angry with us; indeed, people tend to become angrier at someone with whom they are deeply involved.

2. No. Just as negatives from others don't necessarily mean they are rejecting you, a real rejection does not mean that you should reject yourself.

3. Yes. In order to know *who* is wrong, one has to know *what* is wrong.

4. No. The amount of time it takes you to do something is important.

5. Yes. Fine-tuning your ability to handle rejection—learning how to react to it, assess it, and decide to do something about it—is important.

6. No. Most of us *do* set ourselves up, subconsciously at least, for failure ... and would answer this question incorrectly. Those who do recognize this fact, and handle it, would give the correct answer.

7. Yes. Human beings are fallible, and they *do* fail. That's all right, because you must take risks if you are to achieve success, and you

must fail now and then. In order to fail, you must give yourself *permission* to fail.

8. Yes. When you do fail and are reasonably rejected, other factors frequently enter in, so that the feeling of rejection is out of proportion to what it should be. It is important to recognize this and to identify the cause.

9. No. As a rule, the person who has problems in handling rejection also has problems with rejecting properly.

10. No. This question is a bridge toward understanding what rejection objectively *should* be and what it sometimes becomes to us: a sense of loss.

IS YOUR JOB IN JEOPARDY?

It's not difficult to recognize the obvious signs of trouble that can lead to a layoff: the company's earnings are down, budgets have been cut, business just isn't looking good. People probably will be cut, and you could be one of them.

In other cases, there are more subtle signs that could indicate that your job is on the line.

- Your superior doesn't look you in the eye anymore and seems uncomfortable in your presence.
- You no longer are invited to meetings you used to attend.
- An expected pay raise or promotion does not materialize.
- You haven't had any new job assignments lately.
- Coworkers are beginning to avoid you.
- Things seem more strained at work.

Being alert to these early signals can be important. If you move quickly, perhaps you will be able to turn things around and save your job. If that isn't possible, at least you will have more time to negotiate for a more favorable separation package and get an earlier start in looking for another job.

What to do if you suspect your job may be in jeopardy? Generally, it's best to take the initiative, go to your superior, and tell him or her that you're concerned about your job security.

If your superior tells you your job is safe, you have nothing to worry about. Forget the tension you have been under and begin to look for other things that may have caused the "odd behavior" that aroused your suspicions. Chances are, you will discover some other problem, considerably less serious than you had feared, that needs to be resolved.

THE PHILOSOPHY OF SELF-APPRAISAL

Self-appraisal is a vital key to participative management. When we share the burden of appraisal with our superiors, we approach the performance review with a significantly different attitude. When invited, urged, and assisted by the procedure to appraise our own performance, our appraisals are colored by the knowledge that we play a vital role in shaping our own destinies. In actuality, we do and should assume such a role as a participating member of the management team.

Other appraisal systems—in which the individual is called in, allowed to read a completed and agreed-upon review, and informed of his or her status (no questions asked or tolerated)— often leave a feeling of futility, frustration, and antagonism toward the superior and the organization.

We grow and learn through experience on the job. It is easy to become so involved in the day-to-day process of getting the work out, however, that we have little time or inclination to study and analyze what we have been doing. The self-appraisal element of the performance review forces us to study, analyze, and give self-critical attention to the work of the past year. We gain new insights . . . and we continue to grow.

Unfortunately, the word *negotiation* has become tainted through popular usage. We can negotiate with each other without animosity, militant aggressiveness, or other forms of strife often associated with the word. We are management. We must manage; and negotiation is a management process.

There is no such thing as an easy performance review. It continues to be one of the most difficult responsibilities of all managers. It is, however, one of the most fundamental and potentially the most productive of all the manager's duties. While there is no easy way to approach this job, the philosophy of self-appraisal opens the door to a satisfactory review with a minimum of difficulty.

When objectives have been set by the individual and agreed to by the supervisor, we have laid the groundwork for appraising results, not personality traits. If we have gone farther and have agreed on the relative importance of each objective, we have an even stronger basis for evaluation. This type of appraisal measures not only the result we have achieved, but the quality of our objective-setting program, our communications, and our ability as a professional manager.

PERSONAL DEVELOPMENT GOALS

Once the job-related goals have been established, it is easy to move on to a suggested course of action which involves personal development goals.

From your own perspective, these are goals that you must set *for yourself* if you are to become more successful. As a manager, they are the goals you must establish to assist in the development of the personnel under your supervision. The goals are essentially the same; only the level of sophistication is different.

When setting these goals, it is important to be as specific as possible about such things as courses to be taken, publications to be studied, and so on.

Some recommended goals for personal growth and development include:

1. A specific job assignment that will broaden knowledge or experience (for example, temporary appointment as an acting department head).

2. Reading (books, magazines, reports, research publications, etc.)

3. Courses, workshops, seminars, training programs.

4. Management development programs, having determined whether a highly concentrated area of one of two topics or a broad orientation is needed.

5. Programmed instruction.

6. Correspondence courses.

7. Association memberships and professional group activities at either a local, regional, or national level.

8. Giving papers, writing articles, publishing a book.

9. Field trips to other organizations.

10. Attendance at meetings within the organization which the individual normally would not attend.

11. Committee work, especially chairing a group.

12. Individual instruction, such as a one-on-one relationship with someone acting as his or her understudy.

As an exercise, think of one of your own personal development needs. Work out a plan of action in Table 2-5 to help meet the need. Be precise about what work to do, what courses to take, what to read, etc. Start with yourself!

Table 2-5. WORKSHEET—PERSONAL GROWTH OBJECTIVE

I think I need to grow in:

_____

_____

_____

My reason for this belief; my justification for working in this area is: _____

_____

_____

My major concern is one of (check one):   knowledge _____

              attitude _____

              ability _____

This deals with growth in (check one):

      my profession _____

      my management career _____

      myself as a total person _____

Table 2-5. WORKSHEET—PERSONAL GROWTH OBJECTIVE (continued)

NEED

_____

COMMITMENT I intend to make as a means of meeting the need:

_____

_____

HOW my superior and I can tell whether the effort has helped me grow:

_____

_____

_____

Personal growth is important. As Oliver Wendell Holmes once put it: "Even if you are on the right track, you will get run over if you just sit there."

SELF-APPRAISAL
VERSUS TRADITIONAL APPRAISALS

The route to success in management begins with meeting objectives, but it goes far beyond that. Sooner or later, the process of self-appraisal must emerge as the pivotal key. Self-appraisal is basic to the individual's growth plan.

Self-appraisal:

- places the development burden on the individual.
- answers employees' two most basic questions: "How am I doing?" and "Where do I go from here?"
- provides the basis for agreement on priorities.
- improves effectiveness (as opposed to efficiency) in the individual's present position.
- encourages objective analysis of qualifications and relationships.

- relates progress to performance: "Are we doing the right things, and are we doing the right things right?"
- Assists in preparation for added responsibility.

We are often reluctant to work toward effective self-appraisal systems because we are unwilling to start with ourselves. When we do face up to this responsibility, another truth becomes evident: As managers become more objective and realistic about evaluating their *own* progress and performance, they simultaneously become more objective and realistic about the progress and performance of their subordinates.

The Step-by-Step Procedure

Why take the time to review formally the performance of an individual?

1. To try to improve performance on the job now held.
2. To develop people (and let it be known that this is a primary concern).
3. To provide continuity of understanding, and agreement on priorities and objectives.
4. To provide a basis for coordinating organization, unit, and individual objectives.
5. To provide necessary documentation for appropriate personnel actions.

These needs can be met by following four steps:

1. *Employee self-appraisal.* Just prior to the time for an appraisal interview, each individual should prepare a summary evaluation that includes:
   a. Objectives agreed upon at the beginning of the year.
   b. Results achieved for each objective.
   c. Extenuating circumstances relating to any objective that is not met.
   d. Accomplishments beyond previously agreed-upon goals.
   e. Areas for personal growth and improvement, and preparation for future career development.
2. *Supervisor's tentative evaluation.* At about the same time, the supervisor should make an independent summary judgment about the past performance of the individual. This should cover the same points, plus

a summary judgment evaluating the overall contribution of the individual to the organization, but it should NOT stress personality traits.

3. *One-on-one interview.* During this interview, the supervisor compares notes with the individual about progress, performance, and potential. These guidelines are important:

   a. Plan the interview carefully.

   b. Establish a friendly atmosphere.

   c. Let the employee talk first and present the summary he or she has prepared. Encourage personal analysis of performance in order to determine how to build on the individual's strengths and cope with his or her weaknesses.

   d. If necessary, take the initiative, as a counselor, to help the individual with his or her analysis.

   e. Concentrate on the positive aspects of the individual's performance and offer constructive criticism that points the way to future development.

   f. Keep the discussion on measurable results.

   g. Prepare objectives for the next operational period.

   h. Get a commitment about work to be done to satisfy the employee's personal development needs.

   i. Be willing to modify your preliminary judgments about performance if the employee presents new information or insights.

   j. Share everything with the individual, even if agreement is not complete. Work toward a good "batting average" on agreement.

4. *Follow up during the year.* Establish and maintain a performance file on each individual. To assist in making a meaningful appraisal the next time around, place pertinent information (memos, reports, revised objectives, unusual achievements, interviews, etc.) in the file throughout the year.

SELF-APPRAISAL INVENTORY

Before his or her next appraisal interview, each manager should take two or three hours to answer the following questions. Think carefully about each question in sequence. Prepare a preliminary draft of your answers before executing the final version to be discussed with your supervisor.

1. In order of priority, list the top six or eight things which you and your boss agreed you were supposed to get done this year.

2. Beside each of those "accountabilities," write the basis of measurement that was to be used—quantity, quality, time, cost, numbers, dollars, percentages, etc.

3. For each "accountability," give an honest account of how you did in meeting each objective.

4. List every major dissatisfaction that you have regarding your performance during the year.

5. Beside each "dissatisfaction," indicate whether or not you believe your boss agrees, and why.

6. List your most important assets in performing the job you now hold.

7. Beside each "asset," indicate whether or not you believe your boss agrees, and why.

8. On a scale of 1-10, rate your chances of being selected for your present job if you had to reapply for it in open competition. Explain why.

9. Would you want to reapply for your present job? If not, why not?

10. What are the areas of personal development in which you need the most improvement this year? Next year? Over the next three years? Over the next five years?

11. Specify your action plan for achieving that improvement within the specified time frames.

12. List everything you can about what you have learned in your work during the past year and how that knowledge will help you most in the future.

13. Beside each item listed for the previous questions, indicate whether you think your boss agrees. Why or why not?

14. List ways in which your immediate supervisor can help you do a better job. Would the boss agree? Why or why not?

15. What would you most like to see changed about the way your department is run? What change would you suggest? How could the change be accomplished?

16. Other than your present assignment, what would you be qualified to do in your company? Would your present boss agree? Why or why not?

17. If you were to leave your present assignment, who would you nominate as your successor? What are his or her qualifications? Would your present boss agree? Why or why not?

SELF-STUDY QUESTIONS FOR MANAGERS

The following series of quizzes will help you to take an objective look at yourself. Honesty is of prime importance; there is no benefit to being dishonest with yourself.

For each question, score yourself according to the following scale:

Definite Weakness	1-2
Rarely Effective	3-4
Average Performance	5-6
Moderately Effective	7-8
Definite Strength	9-10

Use the chart in Table 2-6 to prepare your composite score.

I. Management style

1. I am sensitive to the influence my actions have on my subordinates. _____
2. I understand their reactions to my actions. _____
3. I find an appropriate balance between encouragement and pressure. _____
4. I allow subordinates to express ideas and opinions. _____
5. I am effective at motivating subordinates. _____
6. I am able to resolve conflicts in a constructive way. _____
7. I have developed a spirit of teamwork among my subordinates. _____
8. I have a clear understanding of my role in the organization. _____
9. I am tactful in disciplining a subordinate. _____
10. I have a personal plan for a self-improvement. _____

SECTION TOTAL _____

II. Planning

1. The operations of my organization are balanced, so that the pace of change is neither too routine nor too disruptive. _____

2. I sufficiently analyze the impact of a particular change on the future of the organization. _____

3. I am sufficiently well-informed to pass judgment on the proposals made by my subordinates. _____

4. I schedule my meetings appropriately. _____

5. My meetings are well planned in advance. _____

6. I have a clear view of the direction for my organization. _____

7. Plans are in written form to guide others as well as myself. _____

8. I make plans explicit enough to guide other's decisions sufficiently. _____

9. They are flexible enough to be changed if necessary to meet the changing needs of the organization. _____

10. The day-to-day work in my unit runs smoothly. _____

SECTION TOTAL _____

III. Information and communication

1. I have good sources of information and methods for obtaining it. _____

2. My information is organized so that it is easy to locate and use. _____

3. I have other people do some of my scanning for me. _____

4. I make good use of my contacts to get information. _____

5. I balance information collecting with action taking. (I have what I need when I need it.) _____

6. My people have the information they need when they need it. _____

7. I put things in writing so that my subordinates are not at an informational disadvantage. _____

8. I use the different media (phone, memos, meetings) appropriately. _____

9. I make the most of meetings for which I am responsible. _____

10. I spend enough time touring my organization to observe first-hand results being accomplished. _____

SECTION TOTAL _____

IV. Time management

1. I have a time-schedule system. _____

2. I avoid reacting to the pressure of the moment. _____

3. I avoid concentrating on one particular function or one type of problem just because I find it interesting. _____

4. I schedule particular kinds of work at special times of the day or week to take advantage of my own energy/effectiveness levels. _____

5. I am in control of the amount of fragmentation and interruption in my work. _____

6. I balance current, tangible activities with time for reflection and planning. _____

7. Key problems/priorities receive the attention they deserve. _____

8. I make use of time-saving devices, such as dictation machines and calculators, when appropriate. _____

9. I have my priorities clearly in mind most of the time. _____

10. I have the necessary information available to me at the right time to meet my deadlines. _____

SECTION TOTAL _____

V. Delegation

1. My subordinates understand our objectives and know what is to be done, when, how well, and by whom. _____

2. I know which of my responsibilities I must meet myself and which I can delegate. _____

3. I encourage initiative in my subordinates. _____

4. I leave the final decision to subordinates often enough. _____

5. I avoid doing the work of my subordinates. _____

6. I show genuine interest in the work my subordinates are doing. _____

7. I am confident that my subordinates can handle the work I give them. _____

8. I give subordinates the guidance, training, and authority they need to make decisions independently. _____

9. I regularly assess the quality of my work and that of my subordinates. _____

10. I use delegation to help my subordinates gain new skills and grow in the organization. _____

SECTION TOTAL _____

GRAND TOTAL OF ALL FIVE SECTIONS _____

Table 2-6. MANAGEMENT SELF-STUDY ANALYSIS—COMPOSITE SCORES

SCORE

Section	10	20	30	40	50	60	70	80	90	100
Management Style										
Planning										
Information-Communication										
Time Management										
Delegation										
TOTALS										

÷ 5 = [ ] Composite Score

Composite Scoring

Draw a line connecting all scores.
Use variations to determine where improvement effort should be concentrated.
Add totals at bottom of each column and divide grand total by 5 to get Composite Score.

If Composite Score is:

80-100:	Strengths should serve you well if exploited.
60-80:	Unbalanced skills may seriously retard your progress.
Under to:	You may be mismatched as a manager.

(Example)

SCORE

Section	10	20	30	40	50	60	70	80	90	100
Management Style					X					
Planning						X				
Information-Communication							X			
Time Management						X				
Delegation									X	
TOTALS					50	120	70		90	330

÷ 5 = 66   Composite Score

This score range	Means:
80-100	Strong area—build on it!
60-80	Aceptable but could be improved.
40-60	Weak area—face up to it!
Under 40	Expect trouble if not improved soon.

Managing People

To test your assumptions regarding people, their work, and how to get them to do the work that is expected, the following quiz will be helpful. Simply check the appropriate column beside each of the fifteen statements that are presented. Read each statement and *immediately* place a check in one of the four columns. Your assumptions are being measured here, not your carefully reasoned responses; therefore, answer at once, not after "qualifying" the statement or looking for the "right" answer. In this quiz, there are no right or wrong answers, and the "best answer is the one that describes what you actually believe; others will only cloud the picture we are trying to obtain—your instinctive pattern of behavior.

Think of "people" in a rather general sense, not as specific individuals. You are trying to analyze your *general* pattern of behavior—the image that you project to others.

It should take you no more than three or four minutes to complete the quiz.

	Strongly disagree	Disagree	Agree	Strongly agree
1. Almost everyone could improve their job performance considerably if they really wanted to.	___	___	___	___
2. It is unrealistic to expect people to show the same enthusiasm for their work as for their leisure activities.	___	___	___	___
3. Even when given encouragement by the boss, very few people show the desire to improve themselves on the job.	___	___	___	___
4. If you give people enough money, they are less likely to worry about such intangibles as status or recognition.	___	___	___	___
5. When people talk about wanting more responsible jobs, they usually mean they want more money and status.	___	___	___	___
6. Because most people don't like to make decisions on their own, it is hard to get them to assume responsibility.	___	___	___	___
7. Being tough with people usually will get them to do what you want.	___	___	___	___
8. A good way to get people to do more work is to crack down on them once in awhile.	___	___	___	___
9. It weakens people's prestige whenever they have to admit that a subordinate has been right and they have been wrong.	___	___	___	___
10. The most effective manager is one who gets the				

	Strongly disagree	Disagree	Agree	Strongly agree

results expected, regardless of the methods used in handling people.

11. It is too much to expect that people will try to do a good job without being prodded by their boss.

12. The boss who expects people to set their own standards for performance probably will find that they don't set them very high.

13. If people don't use much imagination and ingenuity on the job, it's probably because relatively few have much of either.

14. One problem in asking for the ideas of subordinates is that their perspective is too limited for their suggestions to be of much practical value.

15. It is only human nature for people to try to do as little work as they can get away with.

TOTAL FOR EACH COLUMN

"WEIGHTING" EACH COLUMN   ×1_____   ×2_____   ×3_____ ×4_____

TOTAL SCORE

Total the number of marks in each column. Obviously, unless you have skipped a question, the four totals should add up to 15.

Now "weight" your answers by multiplying each column total by the figure given (that is, the total in the *strongly disagree* column × 1; the *disagree* column total × 2; the *agree* column total × 3; and the *strongly agree* column × 4). Enter the answers at the ends of the appropriate columns.

Add the four "weighted" column totals together to obtain your total score. If you have not made any mathematical errors, the figure will be somewhere between 15 and 60.

Now determine where your score would fall in Table 3-1, record it there, and circle it.

Table 3-1.

Style	60 A	Autocratic	33-30 M	Developmental	15 D
Often called . . .		Boss		Leader	
Motivates from . . .		Fear		Inspiration	
Supervision is . . .		Close		General	

The line from A to D on the chart provides for all possible sets of assumptions regarding people and their work. The segment from A to M represents various degrees of autocratic or authoritarian management styles, while the segment from M to D covers differing levels of democratic or developmental supervision.

The theory is that your assumptions about people and their work leads you to develop a certain style of management. The autocrat thinks that people have little ambition, try to avoid responsibility, and want to be told what to do at all times. This leads the manager to assume the responsibility for setting objectives, and causes him or her to exercise close control to see that these objectives are reached. It fosters a relationship in which subordinates are quite dependent, showing relatively little self-expression or self-responsibility. In this climate, participative decision making is rare.

Developmental supervision, on the other hand, challenges people with real opportunity and encourages them to excellence in their performance. It looks upon people as accepting and even enjoying their work, and eager to accept responsibility. It leads to participation in the setting of objectives and to the exercise of broad control that allows people to grow by monitoring themselves. It fosters a relationship in which subordinates can be quite independent and self-reliant if their temperaments allow.

The autocratic manager:
- Says little unless something is wrong.
- Usually is not interested in the ideas of others.

- Decides what information people need.
- Changes demands unexpectedly.
- Is sometimes hard to talk to.
- Discourages people from taking risks.
- Sets objectives *for* subordinates.
- Personally determines performance standards.

The developmental manager:
- Considers ideas that conflict with his or her own.
- Allows a reasonable margin for error.
- Tries to help others learn from their mistakes.
- Has consistently high expectations.
- Encourages people to reach in new directions.
- Helps people understand the objectives of their jobs.
- Allows people to make their own commitments.
- Sets objectives *with* people.

"Pure" autocrats or "pure" developmental managers are rare. Most managers fall somewhere along the line between. The individual circumstances in a situation may dictate how you will react at that moment, but your individual management style stems from the general pattern of behavior that you develop over a period of time.

If you scored 39 or higher on the quiz, you're probably somewhat autocratic; 29 or less, somewhat developmental. If your score was between 29 and 39, you don't have strong leanings one way or the other, therefore your managerial style may vary between the two.

This quiz reflects the impressions others have of you. Does it agree with the image you have of yourself? If not, you may have some problems. At the very least, you may not have the same perception of yourself that others do. Beyond that, you may not know enough about the way in which you deal with people—and why.

If you scored somewhere between 52 and 60, quite a way out on the autocratic scale, you probably tend to be highhanded in dealing with people. You apparently feel that people do not have much initiative of their own, that they have to be watched very carefully, that they have nothing of value to contribute to a group endeavor, and that they are motivated primarily by selfishness. As a result, you probably tend to be too control-oriented in directing their activities.

If you scored somewhere between 15 and 20, rather far out on the developmental scale, you also could be having some troubles. You apparently do not have sufficient sense of the need for controls. Perhaps you are too permissive.

A midrange score of 30 to 33 does not mean that you're necessarily trouble-free. It depends on how you achieved your score. A number of first-column answers, plus a number of second-column answers, resulting in the pluses offsetting the minuses, *could* indicate that you do not recognize the inconsistency of your responses. If one reads the 15 statements very carefully, one will see that all of them really say the same thing, but in a different way. At the very least, you should not strongly agree with some and strongly disagree with others. Answers running down the middle two columns (agree and disagree) really are not inconsistent, given the speed of your response and the absence of any neutral position.

THE IMPORTANCE OF PREPARATION

Tom Landry, coach of the Dallas Cowboys, has a strategy for winning—and it's based on preparation:

"I believe in everything being well planned in my work," says Landry. "No stone should be left unturned. I want to gather all the facts and get all the answers. I relate this information to my coaches, and they relate it to the players. I want to be sure they understand the total picture. I don't want any loose ends that could cause a player to fail.

"In our defensive system [production], everybody has to work together. We rely on planning, preparation, systems, drill and logic, and not much on emotions. In defense, we don't strive for flair, but consistency and logic. We emphasize purpose, planning, and excellence in execution.

"On offense [marketing], we try to use more flair, to achieve a surprise and the unexpected," Landry continues. "Sure, there's a lot of 'show' to it, but there's a purpose to the show. We're try-ing to bring about the result of the opponent's defeat by means of the unexpected, the bold move, the unanticipated surprise stroke. The coach reviews the player's job with him—exactly what he's expected to do. He has precise objectives; he must do certain things to bring results. If he isn't prepared, he'll do the job in an imperfect way that will fail to achieve results. *We do not want any player to fail.* He must feel secure to succeed. If he fails to feel secure, he won't do his best.

"Football is a game of objectives. The Dallas Cowboys play football by objectives. We set team objectives, offensive objectives, defensive objectives, game objectives, and play objectives. Every player has his own objectives."

FROM NONSUPERVISORY PERSONNEL TO TOP MANAGEMENT: HOW SKILLS MUST CHANGE

As supervisory and management responsibilities are assumed, one's skill requirements change. Figure 3-1 shows how those changes would appear graphically.

THE SUPERVISOR AS A TEACHER

A supervisor is someone who moves subordinates from what they already know to a higher level of knowledge and skill, reported *Supervisory Management* magazine in January 1981. The follow-ing eight-point outline describes the role of a supervisor as a teacher:

1. Ask yourself what must be taught. Decide on the skills that need to be learned, and outline the principal points or parts to be taught.
2. Make a chart identifying all the essential skills to be learned, and check off employees who already have mastered each skill.
3. Schedule the time and the place for instruction, and inform the employees. Gather the materials, supplies, tools, and equipment that you will need at the place where the training will take place.

HOW SKILLS MUST CHANGE

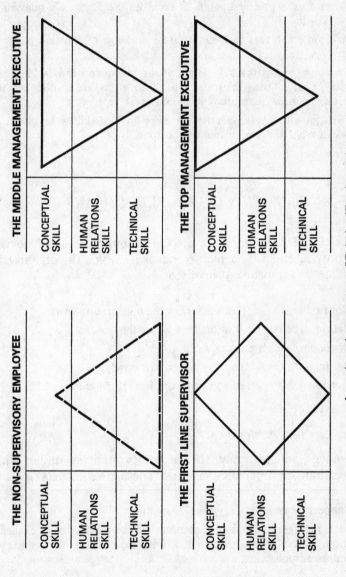

THE NON-SUPERVISORY EMPLOYEE

CONCEPTUAL SKILL

HUMAN RELATIONS SKILL

TECHNICAL SKILL

THE MIDDLE MANAGEMENT EXECUTIVE

CONCEPTUAL SKILL

HUMAN RELATIONS SKILL

TECHNICAL SKILL

THE FIRST LINE SUPERVISOR

CONCEPTUAL SKILL

HUMAN RELATIONS SKILL

TECHNICAL SKILL

THE TOP MANAGEMENT EXECUTIVE

CONCEPTUAL SKILL

HUMAN RELATIONS SKILL

TECHNICAL SKILL

As supervisory and management responsibility is taken, skill requirements change.
Is this diagram consistent with your own views and experience?
If not, why not? What is the most critical step?

FIGURE 3-1

85

4. Prepare the way. What has been the past experience of your employees in learning situations? What do they already know that can be useful in this new situation?
5. Cover all the principal points of your outline. Encourage questions as you go along.
6. Ask the employees to demonstrate knowledge of the skill under discussion.
7. Together, review the key points of the instruction and decide if aids, such as cards listing the main steps of a process, are needed. Together, determine how frequently you should check progress.
8. With the employees, identify the next level of skill to be taught and decide when that should and will be done.

WHAT ORGANIZATION DEVELOPMENT MEANS

Organization Development is the continuing process of devising self-improving and self-correcting means by which the organization will change and improve. It involves:

- Confronting the problems that slow the organization down.
- Getting decisions made at the level where the facts are.
- Developing effective teamwork.
- Dealing with conflicts openly and constructively.
- Increasing awareness of how *process* effects *performance*.

Key Policies for Development

Management must supply the necessary policies under which Organization Development can work. These are some examples:

1. Support by senior management is essential.
2. Each manager and potential manager will be provided with challenges and opportunities for maximum self-development on their present jobs and for advancement.

3. Support will be offered to the entire management group toward the development of skills and competence, which support will be viewed by the company as a future investment.
4. Managers will be provided for the organization in sufficient numbers and diversity to meet future needs.
5. Effective systems will be devised to make it easier for managers to carry out manager development responsibilities.

The Development Process

The process of Organization Development is:

- Identifying able people
- Testing them under fire
- Providing chances for decision making in increasingly difficult situations
- Allowing managers to increase their span of control
- Helping managers develop confidence
- Basing judgment of potential on performance
- Rewarding those who are accountable and take risks
- Providing opportunity for upward mobility
- Encouraging responsibility at the lowest possible level
- Guidance on future performance
- Based upon demonstrated success

The process is *not*:

- Directly related to credentials
- Undertaken *for* someone, but rather *with* him or her
- A social responsibility to underachievers
- A classroom or textbook educational process
- "Educating" as a substitute for "doing"
- A training program
- A single technique
- Placing blame
- A self-fulfilling prophecy

Why Management Development?

Management development is a process of planned managerial learning experiences which stimulate the performance ability of the individual. Management development, through these planned learning experiences, has as its goal to increase the present effectiveness of its personnel and to prepare them for broader managerial responsibility.

Why have management development? Companies retain a management development consultant to assist line management in the development of their people so that *present* managers can help ensure that *tomorrow's* managers will not lose the capability that the present management has built.

It is not something that is nice to do. There is a dollars-and-cents investment involved in management development. Prime reasons for making this investment include:

1. Organizational strength *today*.
2. The need for *continued* organizational strength. Management development assists and assures continuity of good management.
3. For contingency and replacement reasons.
4. Career *retention* of the company's key personnel.
5. Preventing managers from being "indispensable." As long as managers remain the only one that can manage certain departments, there is a probability that they are going to stay in those departments. It is critical to corporate managerial succession that there are backups. A rule of thumb is *two* replacements for every key employee, to provide the company and the immediate organization with sufficient flexibility.
6. The need for diversified experiences.
7. The acquisition of new knowledge and new information.
8. If people are not held accountable for results, they do not grow. If they are not asked to take decision risks or to propose new actions, they do not grow. If they are not given responsibility for results (rather than passively looking on), they do not grow. In the pursuit of development, arrange conditions and provide tasks that release talent potential.
9. The necessity to think through alternatives and make decisions.
10. Developing a process of learning built on errors and success.
11. The opportunity to build relationships.
12. The need to learn the appropriateness of behavior.

ASSESSING ORGANIZATIONAL NEEDS

In order to develop an organization, it is necessary to thoroughly and intelligently assess its needs. Answer each of these questions as it relates to your present position.

1. What does it take to be a good performer in this area?
2. If you were orienting a new employee in this position, what would you identify as key elements for successful performance?
3. What are the major elements of this job that need to be improved?
4. What processes are not being used effectively?
5. What are the consequences of current problem areas and/or poor performance areas?
6. What would you like to see improved in the performance of persons in this department?
7. Are there any organizational policies or practices that hinder good performance?
8. Is poor performance influenced by the organizational structure?
9. What can the organization do to make your job easier?

PLANNING FOR THE DEVELOPMENT OF INDIVIDUALS

Each individual manager has the dual responsibility (1) for personal self-improvement and (2) for creating the best managerial climate for stimulating the self-development of others for whom he or she is directly responsible. The policy must be supported by techniques and methods of high professional quality, which may include:

- A sound organization structure
- Management job descriptions focused on results and management performance standards
- Short-term priority plans which integrate with the organization's plan
- Advanced methods of performance review
- Management training for the individual and for groups, both within and outside the organization

- A management succession plan based on a forward-looking judgment of the scale of the problem
- An equitable salary structure
- Modern techniques of recruitment and selection

COMPETENCE AND PERFORMANCE

There is a close relationship between competence and performance. Competent people achieve goals.

Competence grows when people:

1. Know what is expected of them.
2. Know what they expect of themselves.
3. Know their own limitations.
4. Know where to get help.
5. Can work without direction.
6. Constantly measure their own performance against their own goals.
7. Are comfortable with the idea that rewards will follow achievement.

It was G. W. Grave who said: "There is no future in any job. The future lies in the person who holds the job."

WHY GOOD EMPLOYEES HAVE PROBLEMS

The idea that only poor performers have problems on the job is not true, as chronicled by Jeff Davidson in the May 1980 issue of *Supervisory Management* magazine. Some of the best performers have problems, too, and the reasons are worth considering.

Jealousy: Regardless of the "ideal" employee's intentions, coworkers are ready to believe that this employee is an apple polisher, a traitor, or a "sellout."

Suspicious employers: Many employers are suspicious of an ideal employee and will, in fact, actively seek "clues" as to why the individual is doing such a good job!

Undercompensation: A problem can result when it's time for a raise, and the employee, knowing full well how hard he or she has worked, gets less than was expected.

Exploitation: It is natural for the best employee to be given the toughest assignments, sometimes even when he or she already has a full workload. Ideal employees can easily be taken for granted by their superiors.

Bypassed for promotion: Sometimes an employee is so good at his or her job that the chances for increased responsibility are lessened. Rather than being given the chance to grow, they are relied upon to accomplish current, routine tasks.

Discounted efforts: We all tend to psychologically discount the work done by others—a defense mechanism that keeps us from having to face up to the reality that someone else is doing a better job than we are.

Office politics: The outstanding employee quite often is the last to participate in, or enjoy, the "benefits" derived from office politics.

The truth at all cost: An ideal employee can run into trouble because he or she is unskilled in the techniques of "covering yourself."

WHY EVALUATE PERFORMANCE?

A thorough, serious effort at performance evaluation and potential assessment is difficult, and it says as much about the evaluation process and the organization as it does about the individual being evaluated.

In developing a new system or revising an existing one (and every system should be reviewed after several years), some general guidelines may be helpful.

1. The evaluation technique, instrument, process, and style should be responsive and suited to the needs and style of the particular organization.

2. The organization should be clear as to what it hopes to achieve with an evaluation.

3. To be successful, the system finally adopted should have the support of top management.

4. To achieve credibility, it is wise that those affected, both evaluators and the evaluated, be involved in developing and assessing the evaluation system.

5. The individual who was evaluated should receive a written copy of the evaluation, should have an opportunity to discuss it fully with the evaluator, and should have the opportunity to respond in writing. The evaluation and the response should become part of the individual's personnel file.

6. At least at some levels, the evaluator and his key supervisor should go over the process prior to submitting the evaluation to the one evaluated.

7. To indicate the importance of a careful application of the evaluation system, one of the criteria used by higher executives in judging subordinates should be *their* efforts at evaluating *their own* subordinates.

8. Results should be seen as related to compensation, promotion, job enrichment, and the individual's future with the company.

9. There should be consistency in applying the process and in the high standards set.

10. To ensure all of the above, a successful system needs constant monitoring, concern, and support.

MAKE USE OF THE "WORK ETHIC"

The American work ethic is still strong, but employers are doing little to use it and actually may discourage hard work and attention to quality.

A three-year study conducted by the nonprofit Public Agenda Foundation has pinpointed "a striking failure of managers to support and reinforce the work ethic."

The report is based on interviews with more than 800 working Americans and a review of American management practices in the post-World War II period.

"Our findings suggest that the problem arises from the fact that managerial skill and training have not kept pace with the changes that have affected the work place," the report said. "As a result, the actions of managers blunt, rather than stimulate and reinforce, the work ethic.

"By simplifying and dividing tasks, the technology of the

first industrial revolution made the individual worker less important. The new technology has the opposite effect. The jobs created in a high-technology, knowledge-intensive economy are geared to the skilled and educated employees. The worker becomes more important, and the new technology gives job-holders much more discretion over their own output."

The survey found that 23 percent of the job-holders said they are currently working at their full potential. Forty-four percent said they do not put much effort into their jobs beyond what is required. Nearly 75 percent said they could be significantly more effective on their jobs than they are now.

Bigger paychecks do not reduce this commitment gap. "People need and want money, but money no longer operates as a simple motivator, stimulating people to work harder," the survey said. "Receiving a raise on the job has shifted from being a reward for performance to being an automatic benefit."

BASIC MOTIVATION REQUIREMENTS

In considering the optimum conditions for motivating employees to perform at their highest level, these factors are involved:

Supervisors who:
1. Are approachable and open-minded
2. Share information *before* it is needed
3. Encourage initiative
4. Help people learn from mistakes
5. Give credit when due

A process for setting goals which:
1. Relates organizational goals to personal goals
2. Helps people set goals and measure their own progress
3. Stresses negotiation of results expected in advance

A management system that:
1. Enables individuals to achieve personal goals by achieving organizational goals

2. Can be *managed* by people, rather than stifling them
3. Reveals a developmental rather than an authoritarian approach to supervision

Which of these requirements are met in your organization? Which are *not* being met? Which requirements are not being met in your *unit*? What steps can you take to improve the situation?

WHAT IS YOUR MOTIVATION QUOTIENT?

Key questions to ask in determining the existing level of motivation in your organization include:

1. Is each employee commended when he or she meets specified goals?
2. Does the employer give the employee any recognition (such as a mention in the company newsletter) for long-term service or for retirement?
3. Does the company have a formal awards system to promote excellence?
4. Do senior managers write letters of commendation or otherwise show that they appreciate excellent work?
5. Does the company financially reward an employee who does excellent work? Does it penalized him or her for mediocre work?
6. How many people did the organization reassign or dismiss for poor performance in the previous year?
7. Do supervisors help employees analyze and work out performance problems, or do they merely tolerate them?
8. Are senior managers called in to lend more weight to the importance of meeting required production goals?

Morale and Motivation

What steps can managers take to motivate their personnel and to improve morale? Check those you need to improve.

1. Make greater effort to become more than superficially acquainted with the employees, thereby giving them recognition. ___

2. Improve listening skills, and take more time to listen to the employees. _____

3. Keep employees better informed about what is going on in the organization. _____

4. Do more and better counseling and coaching of employees, and show greater interest in their development. _____

5. Take time to explain why a job or procedure is necessary, in order to impart greater understanding and acceptance of the directions that are given. _____

6. Give credit promptly and sincerely for a job well done. _____

7. Criticize personnel only privately, and be critical only of their job performance, not their personal qualities. _____

8. Invite suggestions for improvement from the employees. _____

9. Consult employees in advance about contemplated changes in order to (a) get their ideas and (b) get them more involved.

10. Use more group problem-solving. _____

11. Let employees know how they will benefit from any changes that are made. _____

12. Delegate more responsibility and authority to subordinates. _____

13. Enlarge and diversify jobs, where practical, to make them more challenging and interesting.

14. Practice management by exception in conjunction with delegation.

15. Use management by objective to improve teamwork and motivation. _____

16. Use performance appraisals as a means of helping individuals improve their effectiveness. _____

17. Encourage and assist subordinates to acquire further education, training, and expertise. _____

18. Try to place yourself in the other person's shoes. _____

Activate or Demotivate?

Remember, people are "activated" when you:

1. Challenge them with important work.
2. Provide necessary support services.
3. Let them know what is expected.
4. Recognize their accomplishments appropriately.

5. Keep them informed of changes that may effect them.
6. Go out of your way to help them.
7. Communicate progress regularly.
8. Face up to needed personnel changes and assignments.
9. Seek their advice sincerely.
10. Demonstrate confidence in them.
11. Encourage ingenuity.

And keep in mind that they are "demotivated" when you:

1. Fail to give them your undivided attention.
2. Fail to acknowledge their personal preferences.
3. Belittle their accomplishments.
4. Criticize them in front of others.
5. Are insensitive to time schedules.
6. Waiver in making a decision.
7. Do not complete your part of the work.
8. Are preoccupied with your own projects.
9. Show favoritism.

What Makes Them Perform?

A few years ago, the United States Chamber of Commerce conducted a study involving 40,000 hourly employees and 5,000 of their supervisors. Employees were asked to rate their job conditions as described below, using a scale from 1 to 10. Their bosses were asked to rank the same items *as they believed their employees would rank them.*

How would you rank these ten items?

Job conditions	*Rating (from 1 to 10)*
Full appreciation of work done.	_____
Feeling "in" on things.	_____
Sympathetic help on personal problems.	_____
Job security.	_____
Good wages.	_____

Work that keeps you interested. _____

Promotion and growth in the company. _____

Personal loyalty to workers. _____

Good working conditions. _____

Tactful disciplining. _____

As a group, the 40,000 employees ranked these items in the following order, from most important to least important:

1. Job security.
2. Good wages.
3. Full appreciation of work done.
4. Feeling "in" on things.
5. Work that keeps you interested.
6. Good working conditions.
7. Promotion and growth in the company.
8. Tactful disciplining.
9. Sympathetic help on personal problems.
10. Personal loyalty to workers.

The 5,000 supervisors, however, said that the workers would rank them in this order:

1. Good wages.
2. Job security.
3. Promotion and growth in the company.
4. Good working conditions.
5. Work that keeps you interested.
6. Personal loyalty to workers.
7. Tactful disciplining.
8. Full appreciation of work done.
9. Sympathetic help on personal problems.
10. Feeling "in" on things.

Note the marked differences in viewpoint. The workers ranked appreciation third, for example, and promotion and growth seventh; their supervisors had the two completely reversed.

Similarly, the workers indicated that it's much more important to feel "in" on things and receive appreciation for work done than their supervisors thought they would. Conversely, the workers thought a lot less of "loyalty" than their bosses thought they would.

If your rankings differ significantly from those of the workers in this survey, it would be a good idea to reexamine how realistic your views are when compared with those of nonsupervisors.

Achievement Eases Stress

Achievement Motivation, the idea of Professor David McClelland of Harvard, has a lot to offer managers in charge of stress-laden organizations. The idea, essentially, is that the level of stress will be acceptable to those caught up in it *if* achievement is present.

A management program built around the major elements of Achievement Motivation would involve:

- Setting goals for the organization and for the people in that organization.
- Speaking the language of success, rather than that of failure. Positive thoughts help people to live with stress. It's better to show confidence and support than to behave in an exacting, critical, hostile, punitive, or judgmental manner.
- Building systems that support success rather than punish failure. Be generous in recognizing and rewarding achievement, and you will get more of it. Praise and rewards are more important in a stress-laden environment than they are in more tranquil ones.
- Building teams to stimulate cooperation, mutual support, and collaboration.

Fifteen Ways to Motivate

It should be remembered that various people respond to different forms of motivation (stimulation) in different ways. Things that succeed with one individual may not succeed with another, even if both are working at the same job, have been with the company an equal time, are the same sex, and are the same age. A good manager will not rely on a single means of motivation but will have an entire "arsenal" of motivational techniques at his or her disposal. Similarly, a successful manager will not consider the motivational responsibility an annual event (sponsoring a yearly sales contest, for example) but will realize that motivation is a day-in, day-out requirement.

Here is a list of fifteen ways in which you can motivate your personnel regularly, consistently, and successfully:

1. Recognize employees for a job well done.
2. Solicit better ideas.
3. Delegate responsibility.
4. Find out what is needed to do a good job.
5. Act quickly on employee complaints.
6. Discipline effectively.
7. Discuss work assignments.
8. Practice fairness.
9. Set a good example.
10. Follow up.
11. Prioritize assignments.
12. Get to know the employees.
13. Build a positive attitude.
14. Present job instructions clearly.
15. Talk to the employees.

Motivating the Underachiever

In modern business, many workers are discontented and maladjusted. Some lack self-confidence and self-esteem and have the idea that management and their coworkers have little confidence in them. As changes occur within an organization, an employee who remains relatively stationary must be afforded new and challenging tasks to avoid the feeling of being bypassed.

The January 1983 issue of *Supervisory Management* magazine offered some ways to bring out the best performance in those who previously have been underachievers:

1. *Instill confidence.* Insecure employees must be praised more often. Such employees always should know when they have done a good job, and should receive this feedback as quickly as possible.

2. *Provide new responsibilities.* Some employees want more responsibility and more independence, but suffer from poor communication ability and interpersonal skills. Training is needed in order to prepare such people to assume additional duties.

3. *Establish authority.* Something in writing often is necessary before some employees will accept it.

4. *Set goals.* The employee needs to identify clearly specific short- and long-term goals for himself and work with management on what needs to be done to achieve those goals. It is the supervisor's responsibility to talk with the employee, to see that goals are set, and to see that steps to reach those goals are planned in detail.

HOW TO BUILD EMPLOYEE COMMITMENT

First, ask yourself: "How committed am I to my overall organizational objectives?" Subordinates cannot provide *your* commitment.

Once you are satisfied with your own level of commitment:

1. Weigh the commitment of your subordinates.
   a. Is it sufficient? (Don't expect them to have the same level of commitment that you do!)
   b. Is commitment obviously lacking?
2. Thoroughly discuss the differences between your commitment and theirs with your subordinates.
   a. How does your commitment to overall organizational objectives differ?
   b. To departmental objectives?
   c. To personal job objectives?
3. Discuss possible action areas, inviting feedback, and agree upon commitment to specific action items.
   a. Commitments made in the presence of peers offer added motivation and communication as well.
4. Hold up your part of the agreement by providing the necessary communication, decisions, and action.
   a. If *you* fail to perform, your personnel cannot be expected to perform.
5. As a part of the ongoing learning process, regularly discuss the progress with your subordinates.
   a. What steps are being taken?

b. Your role.

c. Their role(s).

HOW TO REMEMBER NAMES AND FACES

When you quickly forget people's names, it's not only a waste of time. . . it's embarrassing!

Here are a few exercises to help you remember names and faces more accurately and promptly from Harold Taylor's *Time Management Report*:

1. Be genuinely interested in people—their looks, personalities, jobs, backgrounds, and so on.

2. Listen carefully when someone is introduced. Be sure you hear the name in the first place.

3. If you don't hear the name properly, ask him or her to repeat it and spell it, if necessary.

4. Repeat the name as soon as possible after the introduction. "John Smith. Glad to meet you, John."

5. Keep repeating the name throughout your conversation, and use the name when you part.

6. Try to associate the name of the person with some outstanding physical feature or personality trait. This helps to link the name with the face.

7. When meeting groups, introduce yourself, rather than letting the host or hostess rush through the introductions. Go slowly. Arrive early, so that you can meet people as they arrive.

8. Although it may not be necessary, write the name down when you get a chance.

9. Repeat the name to yourself mentally every so often. As you do so, visualize the person in your mind.

10. Remember that alcohol and memory do not mix.

HOW TO HANDLE PESSIMISTS

Enthusiasm is essential to success. A pessimist often can be converted IF he or she is in full possession of the facts, is kept informed, and is surrounded by people with a positive mental attitude.

Talk the language of goals and success. Talk about challenges and opportunities, not possible pitfalls or "could be's."

Get off on the right foot. Be positive from the outset so that others do not get into the routine of bad-mouthing things and expressing pessimism.

Get your problems laid out and assigned to people. Note the toughest problems and who is assigned to them. A "progress board" on the office wall often helps.

Pay special attention to rewarding innovation and good ideas when times are tough. Nothing boosts optimism like a winning plan, a recovery, a problem solved, or a success.

Watch out for imaginary problems. Ask people to be specific and to focus their energies on corrective action, rather than encouraging them to embellish a real problem with a number of fantasies and imaginary dangers.

Don't take all of the dirty jobs yourself. Pass them out as challenges to your best subordinates.

Watch for symptoms of fatigue. Fatigue can cause an organization to go into a *real* slump. Above all, keep your own energy levels high by getting sufficient rest, by eating properly, and by taking enough time away from the job to renew your mental and physical capabilities.

GUIDES FOR GIVING RECOGNITION

Everyone needs to be refreshed, strengthened, and supported by receiving recognition for a job well done. Suitable recognition for *good work* helps to offset a great many minor *failures* that may have occurred along the way.

1. Praise, reward, and reinforce good performance face-to-face and in public.
2. Provide *negative* recognition face-to-face and in private. Do not punish an employee in public. Don't generalize; attach the specific punishment or reproof to specific behavior. Don't punish every mistake; withholding praise or standing silent on smaller matters can be effective. Be careful

not to punish the right behavior and reward the wrong, which a number of bosses seem to do unconsciously.

3. Have the recognition immediately follow the behavior. The faster the recognition comes, the stronger its effect on the receiver.

4. Large amounts of recognition generally have better effects than small amounts.

5. When a ranking individual uses recognition skillfully, those at lower levels tend to acquire some of that skill.

6. Although it may be impossible to recognize every single item of behavior, fixed schedules for recognition, through monthly meetings and annual banquets, will keep favorable effects alive and well.

7. Don't consider it a waste of time to recognize good behavior. It pays off handsomely in future performance.

HOW TO KEEP YOUR BEST PEOPLE

Good people are the backbone of your organization. They also represent a substantial investment to your company in training and development.

Recognizing this, other organizations—both inside the company and outside it—frequently attempt to lure good people away. Their "bait" comes in many forms.

Good employees will be hesitant to leave *if*:

- You focus on their performance and not on their seniority.
- You don't make your work rules too rigid.
- You avoid arbitrary cutbacks.
- You provide opportunity for personal growth, and avoid dead-end jobs.
- You avoid providing vague goals.
- You reward real accomplishment and not mediocrity.

FAILURE VERSUS MISMATCH

Avoiding failure is different from achieving success. We can avoid failure by simply not trying. In my consulting work, I have observed that most of what is called failure is not caused by people who are *personal* failures but by people who are mismatched at work. That is, their ability to accomplish has been thwarted by personality or behavior barriers *in this situation.* Given other players and a different setting, they may succeed very well. *Moral:* Select the players for each situation with as much evidence of behavior tendencies as you can possibly gather.

SIX WAYS
TO IMPROVE TEAMWORK

People working together as an effective team can accomplish far more than the same number of individuals working separately. Teamwork also improves communication, increases motivation, and stimulates innovation.

To improve your organization's teamwork:

1. *Stress team goals.* Emphasize a common purpose.
2. *Let your people in on your goals.*
3. *Focus on cooperation.*
4. *Show your people how they can help one another.*
5. *Emphasize the importance of each person's job to the success of the group.*
6. *Treat each person as a valued member of the team.*

WHAT TO DELEGATE

The "captain" of the team can't and shouldn't do everything. For greater productivity, as well as the long-term development of competent people, certain tasks must be delegated to individuals or teams throughout the organization.

What are the best tasks to delegate?

1. Problems or issues that require exploration, study, and recommendations for decision.
2. Activities that come within the scope of the subordinate's job and abilities.

3. Tasks that tap human talent in a positive direction, toward organization goals and needs, as well as the individual's growth and development.

4. Problems or activities which, if well handled by the subordinate, can conserve the boss's valuable time.

On a notepad, list some of the tasks or activities within your organization that should be considered for delegation. To whom could it be delegated? What training, authority, help, and/or deadlines would be required? Is there any reason why the task or activity should *not* be delegated?

Delegation: Don't Misuse It

Effective delegation probably is your strongest tool for improving productivity. But in many organizations, delegation is either neglected or misused according to the February 1, 1982, issue of *Boardroom Reports*. Harried, overworked managers are a tip-off that delegation is lacking.

Delegation can improve productivity in three ways:

1. An executive's own time is saved by having subordinates to whom tasks can be given.

2. Subordinates gain motivation, skill, and efficiency as they are given broader responsibilities.

3. Fewer levels of management may be required.

Delegation means different things to different people. Managers should be explicit as to what *degree* responsibility is being delegated to a subordinate. Does one, for example:

1. *Give full authority* to the subordinate to make the decision, with no interference from or consultation with the boss?

2. *Delegate decision making* to the subordinate but ask to be kept informed so there will not be any surprises and so the decision can be coordinated with other people who may be affected?

3. *Require the boss's approval* before the subordinate implements the decision?

4. *Let the subordinate* present alternative solutions but leave the decision making to the boss?

5. *Retain the decision-making authority* but consult first with the subordinate?

You must *learn* to let go of some responsibilities. Be willing to allow failure. Step in only when a poor decision is going to be very costly, either to the company or to the subordinate's career. People do not take responsibility or learn from their mistakes if they always are being second-guessed.

WHAT NOT TO DELEGATE

When making a decision as to what projects should be delegated and to whom, a prudent manager realizes that there are a number of things that he or she should *not* delegate to others. These include:

1. Planning; setting plans within larger plans and objectives.
2. Dealing with morale problems of considerable importance to the work unit.
3. Coordinating line and staff members in reconciling their differences.
4. Coaching and developing the manager's direct subordinates. This is an official—and personal—responsibility that belongs to the manager and should *not* be passed along to someone else.
5. Reviewing the performance of subordinates within one or two levels of the manager.
6. A direct assignment that the manager has been given *by his own boss*.
7. A significant or confidential part of a committee or task force assignment that the manager has assumed.
8. Only *part* of a problem, when the manager or someone else is working on the *whole* problem.
9. Certain "pet" projects, ideas, or activities *unless* they seriously cut into your larger responsibilities as a manager.
10. Matters on which there just isn't enough qualified talent to delegate them to.

THE GROUND RULES OF DELEGATING

Having decided what to delegate and what not to delegate, there are a number of other "rules" regarding delegation that need remembering.

- Select the person to whom you delegate an assignment carefully and well.
- Remember that *you* retain the accountability.
- Create the feeling of responsibility.
- Make the objective clear.
- Make clear what is being *withheld*, if anything.
- Assign the authority—and the support—to get the job done.
- Agree on standards of performance.
- Develop trust.
- Establish checkpoints.
- Delegate the "what," not the "how."
- Assess the risks and provide for them.
- Encourage independent action.
- Give recognition when deserved.
- Take action when things go wrong.

HOW MUCH DELEGATION IS ENOUGH?

Still concerned about how well you are delegating the work? (Remember: We said delegation is a hard thing to learn!)
Try this little quiz:

	Yes	No
Do you often work overtime?	___	___
Do you take work home evenings and on weekends?	___	___
Is your unfinished work increasing?	___	___
Are daily operations so time-consuming that you have little time left for planning and other important matters?	___	___
Do you have control of all details to have a job done right?	___	___
Do you frequently have to postpone long-range projects?	___	___
Are you harassed by constant unexpected emergencies?	___	___
Do you lack confidence in your subordinates' abilities to shoulder more responsibility?	___	___
Do you find yourself irritable and complain when the work of your group doesn't meet expectations?	___	___

Is your work group characterized by conflict, friction, and loss of morale? ___ ___

Do your subordinates defer all decisions to you? ___ ___

Do you instruct your subordinates to perform certain *activities*, rather than to accomplish certain *goals*? ___ ___

Have subordinates stopped presenting their ideas to you? ___ ___

Do operations slow down when you are away? ___ ___

Do you feel that you're abdicating your role as a manager if you ask for your subordinates' assistance? ___ ___

Do you believe that your status and the salary you earn automatically mean that you have to be overworked? ___ ___

If the majority of your answers have been affirmative, it is likely that you are not delegating enough. Work to improve on that weakness, and you will see your organization's productivity increase.

DELEGATION "MUSTS"

As you strive to do a better job of delegation, continually review the following basics.

Understand the need for delegation. You must learn to accept the value and the necessity for delegation, just as your subordinates must do their best to understand their obligations.

Designate goals and objectives. All parties must understand organizational goals and objectives. There should be general agreement on what is to be done, why, how well, when, in what priority, with what resources, and by whom.

Know the strengths of your subordinates. The supervisor should know the characteristics and capabilities of his or her associates and subordinates, then delegate according to those interests and capabilities.

Communicate with your superiors. The supervisor should reach an understanding with his or her superiors as to what is being redelegated.

Negotiate performance standards. Performance standards must be broad enough to encourage individual initiative, creativity, and organizational loyalty. The delegator and the subordinate should agree on them, and preferably in a way that allows the subordinate to feel that he or she is a fully participating member of the decision-making group.

Agree on the areas that are NOT to be delegated. Any exceptions to full delegation should be clearly explained to the subordinate and should be clearly understood to be exceptions, rather than the rule.

Plan for determining subordinates' skills and training. Delegation should include the opportunity for testing employees' skills and for providing any necessary training.

Show your interest. The supervisor should demonstrate a genuine interest in what is being done by his or her subordinates.

Measure the results. Results can be assessed in a variety of ways. Whatever the criterion used, results should be measured regularly and feedback should be provided for the subordinate in such a manner as to allow him or her to "fine tune" his or her performance. This process of measurement also affords all parties an opportunity to reassess or restate their objectives, which aids in keeping the work of the unit "on target" at all times.

Offer help and additional training. Once work has been delegated and the measurement process is in operation, there are naturally occurring situations that call for target setting. The subordinate should play a role in setting those targets, and the supervisor should be alert to opportunities for helping the subordinate to "grow" by providing the necessary training.

WHY MANAGERS FAIL TO DELEGATE

The failure of a manager to delegate often reveals a great deal about the manager and his or her personality and leadership style. To superiors, these revelations may be seen as critical weaknesses . . . and could stand in the way of future advancement.

Why do many managers fail to delegate? There can be a number of reasons, including:

1. *Lack of patience.* How often have you heard someone say: "It takes longer to explain what I want than it does to do it myself"?
2. *Insecurity.* Recently promoted managers often are not comfortable in their new jobs as yet. Sometimes, they simply can't resist the temptation to tell their replacement how to do the job.

3. *Anxiety.* Some managers, especially newly promoted ones, are so anxious to "prove themselves" that they refuse to delegate any part of their work to others.

4. *Inflexibility.* Managers who suffer from this problem are convinced that nothing can be done properly unless they do it themselves.

5. *Inadequacy.* Some people fear to delegate because they are afraid of being "shown up."

6. *Occupational hobby.* Some managers become so attached to a particular part of their work that it becomes a hobby, not just a job. They enjoy it so much they simply don't want to delegate it to anyone else.

Although there are other reasons for failing to delegate, those are some of the most common. If you are not delegating the way you should, does one of them apply to you? More than one? Some other one, not mentioned above?

What can you do to remedy this weakness?

1. Recognize the fault.

2. If possible, try to discover the cause.

3. Practice delegating! Delegation is a skill that is best learned—and developed—through practice.

WHAT WILL YOU DELEGATE?

Try an exercise in delegation.

Some of the following activities may be among your routine tasks. Decide whether you or a member of your staff should handle each one. Consider your total time-management program as you make your decisions.

There are no "correct" answers. The purpose of this exercise is to make you think about using your staff to its full potential and to encourage you to seriously evaluate your own workload.

	Do it myself	Delegate it
Represent your unit in routine meetings.	____	____
Write your speech for a day-long conference.	____	____
Place newspaper ads for a new assistant.	____	____

	Do it myself	Delegate it
Open and sort the day's mail.	____	____
Brainstorm for new ideas.	____	____
Arrange for summer help.	____	____
Read relevant trade journals and books.	____	____
Handle a personnel problem.	____	____
Plan an advertising campaign.	____	____
Talk to a top customer.	____	____
Schedule summer vacations.	____	____
Award maintenance contracts.	____	____
Design and order new stationery.	____	____
Handle routine office personnel chores.	____	____
Officiate at a ribbon-cutting ceremony.	____	____
Line up leaders for a two-day seminar.	____	____
Approve expense accounts for projects.	____	____
Submit a plan for growth in your department.	____	____
Schedule your out-of-town appointments.	____	____
Hire additional stenograph help.	____	____
Give orientation to a new employee.	____	____
Be interviewed for a work-related magazine article.	____	____
Decide on a new intercom system.	____	____
Arrange for sweet rolls for a meeting.	____	____

Take careful note of the number and nature of responsibilities you have retained for yourself. Should you have delegated more? Should you have delegated less?

IMPERATIVES OF INTERVIEWING JOB APPLICANTS

A well-trained interviewer can do more to improve the quality of personnel within an organization than any test yet devised. Objetivity is essential.

Here are some pointers for interviewing well:

1. *Prepare fully for the interview.* Analyze the position and the kind of person needed to fill it. Job descriptions should be in writing. The resume, application, test scores, correspondence, and other relevant material should be reviewed *before* the candidate is admitted to your office.

2. *Use an organized plan for the interview.* Make a brief outline *in advance*, listing the subjects to be discussed and the time available for each. Remain flexible enough to delve into pertinent subjects that may come up.

3. *Take time to establish rapport.* Put the applicant at ease. Establish a climate of mutual trust. Small talk at the beginning of the interview is the usual means of accomplishing this purpose.

4. *Restrain yourself from making a premature decision.* If you rely too much on the initial impression that the applicant makes, the remainder of the interview is largely wasted and there is a tendency to seek out support for your decision rather than to keep an open mind. Important things might be overlooked.

5. *Ask exploratory questions that will get the applicant talking.* Avoid questions that can be answered with a yes or no. Good questions allow for exploration and give the applicant an opportunity to express views or share relevant experiences from his or her background.

6. *Listen.* The interviewee should do most of the talking. You are interviewing the candidate and your role is to listen, analyze, evaluate—and then determine if the applicant is the right person for the job.

Try these suggestions on your next interview. Immediately following, jot down which worked best and which will require further work on your part.

THE TIME AND PLACE FOR COUNSELING EMPLOYEES

Communication is a vital part of your role as a manager. Some of the best communication occurs face to face. Even then, there are certain things you can do to make these sessions more effective.

Pick a time for the counseling session when:

- You are in a good mood.
- You believe the other person(s) to be in a good mood.

- Your relationship with that person(s) is at its friendliest.
- You are not rushed.

Avoid a time when:

- The person with whom you are meeting has suffered some glaring failure.
- The person has recently had some disagreement with you or with some other supervisor.

Hold the meeting where:

- You will not be interrupted, either by someone else or by the telephone.
- You both (all) can be comfortable and relaxed.

Looking back, can you recall situations where these points were neglected and serious problems resulted?

Counseling Guidelines

Counseling sessions can be most productive when they are planned, rather than impromptu.

1. *Let the employee know what's expected.* Clearly define job duties and responsibilities. Discuss standards of performance.
2. *Let the employee know how he or she is doing.* Appraise performance against standards. Get mutual agreement regarding the gap between the actual level of performance and expectations, if there is one.
3. *Develop a plan for improvement.* Have the employee assist in developing the plan. Agree on the plan *together.* Orient the plan to a single job weakness, rather than trying to develop a cure-all that may be too elaborate, too difficult to administer, or too hard to monitor.
4. *Help the employee implement the plan.* Observe the employee's performance and improvement. Praise that improvement, and encourage new efforts. Constructively correct failures. Teach by example. Review progress periodically with the employee.
5. *Reward the results achieved.* On the basis of improvement or results, either provide or withhold the following rewards: praise, recognition, salary increase, increased responsibilities, and/or promotion.

My suggestion is that you refer to these five points every time you have a counseling session with an employee.

HOW WELL DO YOU LISTEN?

When communication is discussed, most of the emphasis is placed on the "transmission." But the "reception" is just as important.

Do you listen well? Answer the following series of questions as honestly and objectively as you can.

When taking part in an interview or a group conference, do you:

	Usually	Sometimes	Seldom
1. Prepare yourself physically by facing the speaker and making sure that you can hear?	____	____	____
2. Watch the speaker, as well as listen?	____	____	____
3. Decide from the speaker's appearance and delivery whether he is saying something important?	____	____	____
4. Listen primarily for ideas and underlying feelings?	____	____	____
5. Determine your own bias, if any, and try to allow for it?	____	____	____
6. Keep your mind on what the speaker is saying?	____	____	____
7. Interrupt immediately if you hear a statement you feel is wrong?	____	____	____
8. Make sure, before answering, that you have taken in the other person's point of view?	____	____	____
9. Try to have the last word?	____	____	____
10. Make a conscious effort to evaluate the logic and credibility of what you hear?	____	____	____

Here's how to score your responses: On questions 1, 2, 4, 5, 6, 8, and 10, give yourself 10 points for every "usually," 5 points for every "sometimes," and nothing for every "seldom." On questions 3, 7, and 9, give yourself 10 points for every "seldom," 5 points for every "sometimes," and nothing for every "usually."

Obviously, a perfect score is 100, and you can assess yourself on that well-known scale. But do not settle for a point grade; instead, look at the questions you answered poorly and resolve to do better in those areas in the future.

Listening: The Key to Understanding

It's normal for your mind to wander when you listen to someone talk. According to the February 1, 1983, issue of *Boardroom Reports*, people normally talk at a rate of 100 to 150 words per minute, and your mind customarily goes at about four times that rate.

To become a better listener, therefore, requires a bit of concentration. Take some extra time to analyze and evaluate what is being said *while* it is being said.

These additional pointers may help:

- Look for the main points of the talk and direct your thoughts to the conclusions you can draw from them. Gathering and using information in this way IS the learning process.
- Separate fact from opinion. Because your mind is going faster than the speaker's voice, you can analyze what is being said. Being able to differentiate between the facts and the speaker's opinions is crucial to how much you will learn from the talk.
- Listen "between the lines." Get in the habit of asking yourself: "What is the speaker *really* trying to say?"
- Notice the speaker's body language. What do the speaker's facial expressions, gestures, and posture tell you?
- Listen for the speaker's *feelings*, as well as his or her meaning.

When You FAIL to Listen

Failure to listen fully and carefully can lead to any number of common problems, any of which *can* become a disaster. For example, poor listening habits may lead to the risk

- that you misread people's intentions
- that you misinterpret their ideas

- that you confuse the issue
- that you misjudge people's qualifications
- that you get instructions wrong
- that you miss valuable information
- that you jump to the wrong conclusions
- that you antagonize people.

THE QUESTIONING TECHNIQUES

You now understand the critical importance of good listening, but what about the importance of *questioning*?

When dealing with a subordinate's performance problems, for example, the ability to ask the right questions of the subordinate is a basic method by which the subordinate can be made to develop and "grow." It's also an important skill to be added to the abilities of any administrator.

The power of the question lies in the fact that *it compels an answer*. If the right questions are asked, the right answers should be forthcoming. If the wrong questions are asked, naturally you will receive the wrong answers.

Asking has many advantages over telling. For a person to manage effectively, he or she must have adequate information, and in many situations a manager can never know as much about certain problems as his subordinates. Therefore, the more questions a manager asks, and the more information he or she receives in response, the better he or she will be able to make decisions. In some cases, there is *no other way* for a manager to gather vital information than to *ask* for it.

It is important that the manager recognize the value of *asking*, rather than *telling*, and that he or she adopt the convictions that subordinates and associates, because of their unique experience, background, and training, can contribute a great deal of information which he or she vitally needs.

To ask the right kinds of questions, one must:

- Understand the different *types* of questions, their nature, purpose, and use.

- Understand the *direction* of questions, how to channel them and handle them.
- Develop skill and proficiency in using the correct questioning technique in the appropriate situation.

The types of questions, their purpose, and some examples are shown in Table 3-2.

Using another chart (Table 3-3), we can help to develop a cleaner picture of the direction of questions.

Table 3-2. THE QUESTIONING TECHNIQUES

TYPES OF QUESTIONS

Types	Purpose	Examples
1. Factual	1. To get information. 2. To open discussion.	1. All the "W" questions: what, where, why, when, who, and how?
2. Explanatory	1. To get reasons and explanations. 2. To broaden discussion. 3. To develop additional information.	1. "In what way would this help solve the problem?" 2. "What other aspects of this should be considered?" 3. "Just how would this be done?"
3. Justifying	1. To challenge old ideas. 2. To develop new ideas. 3. To get reasoning and proof.	1. "Why do you think so?" 2. "How do you know?" 3. "What evidence do you have?"
4. Leading	1. To introduce a new idea. 2. To advance a suggestion of your own or others.	1. "Should we consider this as a possible solution?" 2. "Would this be a feasible alternative?"
5. Hypothetical	1. To develop new ideas. 2. To suggest another, possibly unpopular, opinion. 3. To change the course of the discussion.	1. "Suppose we did it this way. What would happen?" 2. "Another company does this. Is this feasible here?

Table 3-2. THE QUESTIONING TECHNIQUES (continued)

TYPES OF QUESTIONS

Types	Purpose	Examples
6. Alternative	1. To make decision between alternatives. 2. To get agreement.	1. "Which of these solutions is best, A or B?" 2. "Does this represent our choice in preference to . . .?"
7. Coordinating	1. To develop consensus. 2. To get agreement. 3. To take action.	1. "Can we conclude that this is the next step?" 2. "Is there general agreement then on this plan?"

Table 3-3. THE QUESTIONING TECHNIQUES

DIRECTION OF QUESTIONS

Type	Purpose	Examples
A. *OVERHEAD:* Directed to group.	1. To open discussion.	1. "How shall we begin?" 2. "What should we consider next, anyone?" 3. "What else might be important?"
B. *DIRECT:* Addressed to a specific person.	1. To call on person for special information. 2. To involve someone who has not been active.	1. "Al, what would be your suggestions?" 2. "Fred, have you had any experience with this?"
C. *RELAY:* Referred back to another person or to the group.	1. To help leader avoid giving own opinion. 2. To get others involved in the discussion. 3. To call on someone who knows the answer.	1. "Would someone like to comment on Bill's question?" 2. "John, how would you answer Bill's question?"

Table 3.3 THE QUESTIONING TECHNIQUES (continued)

	DIRECTION OF QUESTIONS	
Type	*Purpose*	*Examples*
D. *REVERSE:* Referred back to person who asks question.	1. To help leader avoid giving own opinion. 2. To encourage questioner to think himself/herself. 3. To bring out opinions.	1. "Well, Dick, how about giving us *your* opinion first?" 2. "Bob, tell us first what your own experience has been."

Questions perform certain *functions* and take certain *forms* in order to get at facts and feelings. Once again, we shall try to illustrate that point with a chart:

Function	*Form*
To identify and isolate	."What?"
To differentiate and separate.................	."Which?"
To locate and specify......................	."Where?"
To single out individuals, groups, or organizations	."Who?"
To specify date and time....................	."When?"
To get reasons, causes, and explanations	."Why?"
To quantify and measure	."How much?"
	"How many?"
	"How soon?"
To encourage suggestions and action............	."How can ...?"
	"Who can ...?"
	"When can ...?"
	"What can ... ?"
	"Where can ...?"
	"Why does ...?"

THE GENTLE ART OF SAYING NO

Having to deny someone's request is psychologically unpleasant, whether the individual making the request is a member of the family or an employee on the job. One knows that doing so invites the person who has been refused to complain to friends and co-workers that one has been unreasonable or unfair. One also knows that, in some sense, a refusal disappoints the employee and thereby hurts him or her.

Still, refusals *must* be made, and the most painless way in which to do it includes three steps:

1. Bite the bullet and *do* it. Say: "No, I cannot [will not] meet your request."

2. Give the individual a reason or explanation for your refusal. This changes his or her possible perception of you as unreasonable or arbitrary.

3. Show the individual that his or her needs are important and that you would like to be able to meet them. If possible, offer an alternate course of action or solution: "I can't meet your request, but I can . . ." This helps the individual to understand your reasons for refusal and overcomes his or her feeling of rejection.

SUBORDINATE GROWTH OBJECTIVES

Helping your subordinates to grow and develop will be a great deal easier if you do it according to some predetermined plan. You will recall that in Chapter 2 we recommended an analysis of *your own* personal development goals, followed by the use of a worksheet to help you formulate a *plan* for reaching those goals. Use of a similar approach for each subordinate will enable you to do a more reasoned, more orderly, and more consistent job of developing your personnel.

Try using the form in Table 3-4, almost identical to the one you did for yourself, as a daily *working* guide.

SUPPORTIVE MANAGERS

Employees respond in much better fashion when they sense (know) that their manager is supportive. Are you? Write yes or no after each of the questions on the following page.

Table 3-4. WORKSHEET—SUBORDINATE GROWTH OBJECTIVE

NAME OF INDIVIDUAL: _____

I think this individual needs to grow in:

_____

_____

_____

My reason for this belief, my justification for sharing it is: _____

_____

_____

_____

My major concern for this individual is (check one):

knowledge	_____
attitude	_____
ability	_____

This deals with growth in (check one):

profession	_____
management	_____
total human	_____

1. Do you start with the assumption that you have good people who are deserving of your trust?
2. Do you have high expectations, and believe that your people will meet or exceed them?
3. Do you state your expectations in advance, clearly, and in terms of objectives?
4. Do you use those objectives as a yardstick for judging results and avoid "changing the rules" in the middle of the game?
5. Do you allow your people to take some risks on the job?
6. Do you stress your employees' strengths over their weaknesses?

7. Do you consult your employees as to what they can do, can do differently, or can refrain from doing in order to do their jobs more successfully?

8. Do you recognize and reward achievement?

9. Do you praise your people publicly and reprimand them privately?

10. Do you set a good example and avoid reminding your people of your authority?

Now, for every no response you should (1) identify the people and/or situations that came to mind, (2) priorities the list, and (3) outline a brief action plan indicating what you plan to do, with whom, and by when.

APPRAISING A SUBORDINATE

The process of evaluating subordinates takes place constantly. This appraisal may be conscious or subconscious, formal or informal, objective or not, fair or not. Obviously, it will be to the manager's advantage, as well as to the employee's, if the appraisal is fair, consistent, reasonably frequent, and performed according to some standard that is mutually understood and (hopefully) previously agreed upon.

Try evaluating each of your employees according to the criteria below. Grade him or her 1-4 if the statement reflects a definite weakness; 5-7 if it reflects average proficiency; and 8-10 if it's an area in which the individual shows definite strength.

Planning

1. Understands job responsibilities and authority clearly. _____

2. Is able to formulate realistic plans and schedules. _____

3. Classifies the work to be done, divides it into components, and creates orderly and productive arrangements. _____

4. Is able to utilize resources (manpower and other) productively. _____

5. Establishes priorities for work to be done, personally and by others. _____

6. Sees to it that each person understands his or her responsibility and authority. _____

7. Plans and conducts effective meetings as required, and avoids unnecessary ones. _____

8. Uses meetings to develop people. _____

9. Shows people how each job fits into the total picture. _____

10. Sees that people have the equipment and materials they need to do their jobs. _____

TOTAL SCORE—PLANNING _____

Initiating

1. Recognizes and corrects situations that need improvement. _____

2. Is able to originate new approaches to problems. _____

3. Makes the most of a promising new plan or idea. _____

4. Puts worthwhile suggestions into operation. _____

5. Encourages subordinates to try new methods and ideas. _____

6. Faces up to problems. _____

7. Begins working on new projects without waiting to be told. _____

8. Seeks solutions, rather than excuses. _____

9. Doesn't hesitate to ask questions to get needed information. _____

10. Is willing to take reasonable risks. _____

TOTAL SCORE—INITIATING _____

Delegating

1. Is able to effectively delegate responsibility and authority at all levels. _____

2. Avoids trespassing on authority, once delegated. _____

3. Periodically checks the performance of others on duties that have been delegated. _____

4. Is concerned with a minimum of detail. _____

5. Tries to define jobs delegated to others so as to provide them with the greatest challenge and opportunity. _____

6. Inspires people with the willingness to work toward objectives. _____

7. Makes full use of the skills and abilities of subordinates. _____

8. Provides the necessary know-how for subordinates. _____

9. Has subordinates participate in setting work objectives and schedules. _____

10. Tries to get group reaction on important matters before going ahead. _____

TOTAL SCORE—DELEGATING _____

Decision making

1. Decisions are consistent with policies, procedures, and objectives of the organization. _____
2. Decisions are consistent with the economic, social, and political climate. _____
3. Keeps within the bounds of authority and ability in making decisions. _____
4. Considers and correctly interprets key facts in solving problems. _____
5. Uses own experience and that of others in reaching conclusions. _____
6. Accepts responsibility for decisions, even when others are consulted. _____
7. Makes decisions promptly, but not hastily. _____
8. Makes decisions that are realistic and clear-cut. _____
9. Takes calculated risks, based on sound decision making. _____
10. Converts decisions into effective and decisive action. _____

TOTAL SCORE—DECISION MAKING _____

Communicating

1. Keeps informed on how subordinates are thinking and feeling. _____
2. Encourages others to express their ideas and opinions. _____
3. Listens with understanding and purpose. _____
4. Responds intelligently to criticisms of own actions. _____
5. Handles questions promptly. _____
6. Keeps people informed on changes, policies, procedures affecting their work. _____
7. Recognizes the good work of others and expresses appreciation. _____
8. Explains the "why" of decision. _____
9. Makes significant contributions to meetings, both listening and speaking. _____

10. Expresses self clearly and effectively in writing and speaking. _____

TOTAL SCORE—COMMUNICATING _____

Developing

1. Selects properly qualified people for jobs. _____
2. Helps new employees adjust to the job and the group. _____
3. Creates in people a desire to do a better job. _____
4. Systematically evaluates the performance of each employee. _____
5. Keeps people informed on how they are doing. _____
6. Uses constructive criticism reflecting a helpful attitude. _____
7. Discusses career opportunities with subordinates. _____
8. Helps subordinates formulate self-improvement plans. _____
9. Informs higher authorities of subordinates' accomplishments and developments. _____
10. Has a plan for self-development and is actively engaged in it. _____

TOTAL SCORE—DEVELOPING _____

Relationships

1. Is firm and fair in dealing with subordinates and associates. _____
2. Is able to "take it" when the going is rough. _____
3. Is able to show enjoyment of work and associates. _____
4. Makes it easy for people to talk. _____
5. Visits subordinates and associates in their offices and workplaces. _____
6. Is interested in the personal well-being of others. _____
7. Understands how off-the-job problems can be related to on-the-job performance. _____
8. Participates appropriately in community activities. _____
9. Tactfully adjusts to personalities and circumstances. _____
10. Sells ideas to others without pressure. _____

TOTAL SCORE—RELATIONSHIPS _____

Performance standards

1. Uses systematic methods to measure performance, productivity, and progress. _____

2. Jointly develops objectives and performance standards with subordinates. _____

3. Evaluates continually to readjust the organization and work standards. _____

4. Sees that standard operating practices are followed when necessary. _____

5. Determines accountability. _____

6. Faces up to failures in meeting standards. _____

7. Does not seek goals that are unreasonably high. _____

8. Does not settle for goals that are too easily accomplished. _____

9. Is willing to negotiate when standards should be changed. _____

10. Helps determine an acceptable range of performance when a precise standard is not necessary. _____

TOTAL SCORE—PERFORMANCE STANDARDS _____

Now transfer the employee's scores to the chart in Table 3-5. Connect the individual's scores with lines, as shown in the example.

If the individual scores between 80 and 100 in a *specific skill area*, it indicates that he or she has a specific strength in that area and should be encouraged to build on it. A score of 60 to 79 means that the level of that skill is acceptable but could be improved. Between 40 and 59, the individual's skill in that area is weak, and he or she should face up to it. Under 40, the individual should expect trouble on the job unless there is improvement in that skill area soon.

Variations in the line you have drawn to connect the various individual skill-area scores will give you a graphic picture of the areas in which the employee needs improvement. The composite score, reached by totaling all of the individual skill-area scores and then dividing them by eight (the number of skill areas tested), may be evaluated in this fashion:

- *80-100:* The employee's combination of skills is good and well rounded. They should serve him or her well, if properly exploited.

- *60-79:* A reasonable "average," but if the score results from several highs and several lows, the imbalance in his or her

Table 3-5.

Skill	SCORE									
	10	20	30	40	50	60	70	80	90	100
Planning										
Initiating										
Delegating										
Decision-Making										
Communicating										
Developing										
Relationships										
Standards										
TOTALS										

(Grand Total _____ ÷ 8 = _____ (Composite Score)

Example

Skill	SCORE									
	10	20	30	40	50	60	70	80	90	100
Planning					52					
Initiating						61				
Delegating							79			
Decision-Making					65					
Communicating						63				
Developing								86		
Relationships									93	
Standards				43						
TOTALS				43	52	189	79	86	93		542

(Grand Total) 542 ÷ 8 = 67.75 (Composite Score)

127

particular job skills could seriously retard this person's progress. Work to bring *all* skill areas to this level, at least.

- *Under 50:* This employee would be mismatched as a manager or supervisor. A great deal of development is needed before he or she can be considered for any significant promotion.

Now that you have evaluated each of your subordinates according to these criteria, you may find it helpful to use them to evaluate *yourself.* Be objective! The findings could be very beneficial.

A RESULTS-ORIENTED PERFORMANCE APPRAISAL

A results-oriented performance appraisal is a system of evaluating performance based on success or failure in meeting predetermined objectives. It requires managers and subordinates to establish performance objectives jointly; then for *both* to evaluate performance with the advice and concurrence of a manager at the next highest level. The system stresses the importance of face-to-face discussion between the manager and the subordinate, both for the purpose of setting the objectives and then for the purpose of evaluating performance.

The objectives of results-oriented appraisal are fivefold:

1. To improve present performance.
2. To develop people for added responsibility.
3. To answer employees' two most basic questions: How am I doing? Where do I go from here?
4. To provide coordination of departmental and individual goals.
5. To determine certain personnel actions, such as a salary increase, a promotion, or a transfer.

The Results-Oriented Performance-Appraisal Interview

Having previously met with the subordinate and developed a clear, measurable, and mutually agreeable set of objectives, you can ensure the performance appraisal will be based upon specific accomplishments. When performance is to be evaluated, it is best done in a face-to-face *interview* involving the manager and the subordinate, following the guidelines listed on page 72. In addition, these key points are very important:

1. Encourage the employee to analyze and appraise his or her performance as a means of determining any areas of weakness and as a means of understanding *why* performance turned out the way it did. Use such questions as: "What do you believe may have caused that project to fail?" and "Why do you suppose you feel this way?"

2. Occasionally, as coach and counselor, you will have to take the initiative and point out why the performance failed or succeeded, what the employee's strengths and weaknesses are, and what improvement is needed.

3. Be sure the discussion stays on specifics.

4. Don't get bogged down in disagreement or argument.

5. Don't try to avoid the year's failure or lack of accomplishment. Listen to the employee's views and, if the facts warrant, recognize the lack of achievement. Remember, however, that last year is history, and center your discussion on what can be learned from it, rather than trying to justify why it happened.

6. Remember at all times that *you* are the manager. Never say "they," as in "I told them how you felt, but they disagreed." Instead, say "We discussed how you feel and reached the conclusion that . . ."

PERSONALITY-ORIENTED MANAGEMENT

When management is more personality-oriented than results-oriented, it opens the door to a number of potential problems:

- People who "fit in" are promoted over people who perform well.
- "Pleasing the boss" may be a bigger factor in promotions than job effectiveness.

Personality-oriented firms often demonstrate certain distinguishable characteristics. Selection is based mostly on psychological testing. Appraisal forms are more concerned with personality traits than objectives. Coaching of managers by their superiors often consists of warnings about the changes in personality that are required to "get ahead." Training programs often are centered on "getting along" and personality adjustments, rather than on productivity and creativity.

If there is evidence of this sort of thinking in your organization, what steps can you take to change it?

CAUSES FOR ERROR IN APPRAISALS

If your organization consistently seems to have a high turnover and, most important, if good people leave and go on to considerable success in other jobs, you have a clear sign that your appraisal system is not working properly. This may be due to one of the following common weaknesses:

- Unwillingness to take the time and effort to do the appraisal thoroughly.
- Giving recent occurrences too much weight when the appraisal is made.
- Personal prejudices or bias on the part of the rater.
- Lack of uniform criteria or job standards.
- A reluctance to point out a subordinate's weaknesses and help him or her to improve on them.

DOUBLE TALK IN JOB-RATING TERMS

Unfortunately, appraisals are often couched in double talk when they should be clear, concise, and specific. Beware of the manager who says one thing when he or she really means another. For example:

This	May really mean
Average	Not too bright.
Exceptionally well qualified	Has committed no major blunders to date.
Active socially	Drinks heavily.
Zealous attitude	Opinionated.

This	*May really mean*
Unlimited potential	Will stick until retirement.
Quick thinking	Offers plausible excuses for error.
Takes pride in work	Is conceited.
Forceful and aggressive	Argumentative.
Indifferent to instruction	Knows more than his or her superiors.
Tactful in dealing with superiors	Knows when to keep his or her mouth shut.
Takes every opportunity to progress	Buys drinks for the boss.
Spends extra hours on the job	Has a miserable home life.
Conscientious and careful	Is scared.
Meticulous attention to detail	Is a nit-picker.
Demonstrates qualities of leadership	Has a loud voice.
Strong adherence to principles	Is stubborn.
Gets along well with superiors, subordinates	Is a crowd.
Of great value to the organization	Turns in work on time.
Unusually loyal	Nobody else wants him or her.
Alert to company developments	Is a gossip.

FOUR TYPES OF PROGRESS REVIEWS

When reviewing the performance of any employee, four distinct areas should be taken into consideration: the Performance Review, the Salary Review, the Career Planning Review, and the Promotion Review.

1. The Performance Review. The manager reviews the subordinates' progress and coaches with reference to:
   a. Actual work accomplishments in comparison with previously agreed-upon goals.

131

    b. Improvement needed.

    c. Support needed.

2. The Salary Review. The manager reviews:

    a. The value of the results achieved by the employee.

    b. The relationship between these results and the organization's salary-administration program.

    c. The results accomplished, as a basis for taking appropriate salary action.

3. The Career Planning Review. The manager counsels subordinates with reference to:

    a. The relationship of interests and aspirations to his or her future.

    b. The employee's present position relative to:

        1. Knowledge and experience

        2. Abilities and aptitudes

        3. Skills and proficiencies

        4. Habits and work relationships

    c. Work done, particularly with respect to opportunities and priorities for improvement.

    d. Personal development in terms of a plan and a program for growth.

4. The Promotion Review. The manager discusses:

    a. Opportunities that may be available in the future.

    b. Possible positions in terms of what results may be required to qualify for them.

    c. Needed qualifications in terms of job performance and personal factors.

TYING APPRAISALS TO OBJECTIVES

Appraisals don't stand alone. They are an integral part of a *total* management system *if* they are effective. To see that they *are* effective, it is important for a manager to:

1. Teach the nature and philosophy of the entire system.

2. Give subordinates adequate tools.

3. Recognize the network nature of the organization and the need for goals.

4. Insist on verifiable objectives.

5. Make goals realistic and attainable.

6. Recognize the timespans necessary to reach those goals.

7. Make goal setting a process of negotiation.
8. Be willing to change goals, when necessary and possible.
9. Institute and maintain a reasonably formal and rigorous review at (a) goal-setting time and (b) appraisal time.
10. Look upon the appraisal as only one element in a system of management by objectives.

APPRAISAL RECORDS

Appraisals should not be the product of memory alone. Nor should they reflect the manager's most recent impression of an employee.

During the course of the year, maintain a file on each of your subordinates as an aid to the next appraisal. Such files should contain memos, reports, notes on revised objectives, and similar information, which might include:

- Successful completion of an objective.
- Initiation or completion of some phase of the subordinate's personal development program.
- Notice of an unforeseen problem that affected performance.
- Notice of developing conditions or factors (new equipment, organizational changes, etc.) that may affect performance.
- Budget and expense reports.
- Outstanding or unusual achievements related to performance.
- Constructive criticism or disciplinary interviews.
- Outstanding or unusual failures in performance.
- Coaching or counseling interviews.
- Revision of objectives.
- Complaints against the employee by his or her own subordinates.

CAUSES OF MARGINAL PERFORMANCE

Obviously, it would be ideal if each employee were to perform to the very limit of his or her capability. Unfortunately, that seldom happens. Sometimes, in fact, the manager must recognize and deal with a subordinate who is barely "getting by."

It is usually helpful in such situations if the manager can determine *why* the employee is not meeting the organization's expectations. What may be *causing* the employee to perform poorly?

Often, the answer is one of these:

1. The supervisor and the employee have failed to reach an understanding as to what is expected. In the employee's mind, he or she may be doing a terrific job!

2. The employee lacks some necessary knowledge or skill and does not know where or how to acquire it.

3. The employee is not challenged by the job.

4. The employee lacks commitment.

5. The employee feels that he or she has too many goals to achieve or that the mixture of goals is impossible to achieve.

6. The employee lacks sufficient feedback from the supervisor as to his or her performance.

7. The employee's work is hampered by an existing process, method, system, or policy.

8. The employee's work is adversely affected by the failure of others to meet their commitments.

Dealing with the Marginal Employee

Managers who are forced to deal with a marginal employee can avoid a great deal of frustration and achieve better results if they will:

1. Clarify the individual's and the organization's goal.

2. Discuss (negotiate) the combination of both goals, thereby satisfying the individual's needs as well as those of the organization.

3. Develop a plan of action that will involve both the manager and the employee.

4. Maintain their (the manager's) end of the agreement and actively encourage the employee's improvement.

5. Continually evaluate what progress is being made.

6. Use a performance chart or keep records so that the employee can see his or her progress.

7. Realize that, if all of this produces no improvement in the employee's progress, Personnel should be consulted and termination procedures should begin.

MAKING EMPLOYEE EVALUATIONS PAY OFF

A good performance appraisal can stimulate an employee's self-motivation and provide the means for improving performance. The manager can maximize the value derived from an appraisal, according to the January 1983 issue of *Training* magazine, by:

- Conducting performance appraisals in private and giving the subordinate his or her undivided attention.

- "Leveling" with the employee by providing specific examples of his or her proficiencies and deficiencies.

- Testing his or her understanding of the employee's concerns by summarizing what has been said.

- Focusing on future improvement and asking the employee for a definite action plan to improve future performance and build on it.

- Explaining development opportunities as well as remedial needs.

- Assuring the employee that the appraisal covers only the current period; that ratings are not labels; and that everyone earns his or her way from one evaluation period to the next.

REASONS FOR A QUARTERLY PERFORMANCE REVIEW

Too often, performance reviews are poorly structured, inconsistent, uncoordinated, infrequent, hit-or-miss propositions. Obviously, one cannot expect to get full value out of such "casual" procedures.

Even the traditional *annual* review may not be sufficient to the needs of a growing organization, operating in a highly competitive marketplace, and operating in an era of rapidly changing socioeconomic conditions.

There are a number of excellent reasons why more frequent, perhaps quarterly, performance reviews may be needed:

1. You can revise any goals that need revising.
2. You can do away with any goals that no longer are relevant.
3. You can recognize achievements while they still are fresh in your mind and in the mind of the subordinate.
4. You can uncover serious problems in an earlier stage, *before* they become large, embedded, and impossible to solve.
5. You can add new goals to exploit recent opportunities.
6. You can adjust your priorities, advancing some projects and deferring others.
7. You can discover new concerns that have arisen in the employee's job or personal life since the last review.
8. You can be more current on the quality of the relationships that occur between the subordinate and other members of the group.
9. You can discover ways in which to be of more help to the subordinate by asking, "Is there anything I can do, can do differently, or can stop doing to help you get your job done?"

ASSESSING YOUR APPRAISAL STYLE

Appraisal "styles" range from that of the manager who takes pride in attempting to change everyone to that of the manager who acknowledges a value in *limited* control.

Four basic styles could be designated, ranging from one in which management is able and responsible to one in which management has little or no control, according to *Supervisory Management* magazine, December 1982. Thus, you can have Developers, Demanders, Resigners, and Avoiders.

Developers: These people see themselves as mentors and are insensitive to the employee. They coach and suggest, and tend to make good workers better, but they are generally not effective with marginal performers.

Demanders: These managers believe it is their responsibility to set goals and believe that their subordinates had better perform. They get the best out of some of their people, but others simply rebel or withdraw. This style can stifle creativity and reduce the employee's self-confidence.

Resigners: These individuals often feel that they lack the support of the organization. Since they feel that they must control everything or they can't control anything, they refuse to exercise the control they do have. They have little use for the appraisal system because they do not believe it is effective. Their cynicism obscures their power over their employees.

Avoiders: Avoiders seek to minimize confrontation. They know appraisals must occur, but they don't want them to get "awkward." They do a fine job of maintaining their perspective, but they often fail to address real problems head-on.

Which type are you? Do you feel that you are getting the most you can from your supervisors/managers? Are you promoting the right people? Are your managers coming up with new ideas? Do you have to do much of your managers' thinking for them? Are there weak links in your managerial chain? Do you and your subordinate managers agree on their major responsibilities? Do you and your subordinate managers have—and agree on—goals? Do you and your subordinate managers do your action planning together? Are you satisfied with your performance-evaluation system?

HOW MANAGERS WANT TO BE MANAGED

Supervisors and managers are motivated by more than money. If you are to stimulate them to perform at top efficiency and optimum effectiveness, you must be aware that they also want:

- To know what is expected of them.
- To know how to get ahead.
- To participate in decision making.
- The necessary resources to do their jobs.
- Freedom to operate.
- Feedback.
- Bosses who listen.

- Information.
- Fair and courteous treatment.
- Financial equity.
- Appropriate status.
- Effective role models.
- Recognition of their ability.
- Reward for their efforts.

THE BOSS'S PERSONALITY

Understanding the personality of your boss—and *your own* as someone else's boss—helps you to understand why they (and you) react the way they do (you do) in certain circumstances.

Can you identify your boss (yourself) among the following?

Action-oriented supervisor: A common type. A dynamo who works himself or herself and employees hard; makes quick, effective decisions (which may ride insensitively over subordinates' feelings); and is happiest with tight deadlines and dramatic results.

The "default" boss: Courts you until you're hired and then deserts you once you're on the job. He doesn't train, instruct, develop, or encourage and is ill at ease with people and most comfortable with statistics, budgets, research findings, and technology. If you don't "work out," he or she simply lets you go.

The M.B.A. manager: Totally enrapt when quantifying business data and problem solving. Those who succeed best with them are those who concentrate on being pragmatic and demonstrate their ability to plan, work, and think in functional terms toward ever-evolving business objectives.

The founder: Operates on a plan-as-you-go basis and expects you to adapt. The business is his or her "baby," so this boss is slow to delegate and tends to renege on commitments or override you constantly.

The survival boss: Wants, above all, to avoid risks. Makes decisions on the basis of the safest course. Difficult to work under if you are aggressive, ambitious, creative, or feisty.

The leader: Can listen, respect others and their ideas, get to the root of a problem, draw correct conclusions from data, make clear decisions, and be sensitive and considerate toward people. Values subordinates' talents and contributions, and rewards accordingly.

RATING YOUR BOSS AS A LEADER

What kind of person do you work for? You will have a little better idea once you have rated him or her according to the following scale, developed by Robert Townsend in his practical book *Further Up the Organization*. Score each element from 0 to 10.

My boss is:

1. *Informative.* Quick to let me in on information which might be useful to me, or stimulating, or of long-term professional interest.   _____

2. *Objective.* Negotiates goals. Determines priorities. Monitors progress. Knows what's *really* important from what *seems to be* important.   _____

3. *Effective.* Teaches me to learn from my mistakes as he or she does.   _____

4. *Decisive.* Gets quickly to the decisions which can tie up an organization for days.   _____

5. *Available.* . . . if I have a problem I can't solve. But forceful in making me do my best to bring in solutions, not problem.   _____

6. *Fair.* Concerned about me and what I'm doing. Gives credit where credit is due, but holds me to my commitments.   _____

7. *Tough.* Won't waste time. Is more jealous of subordinates' time than his or her own.   _____

8. *Patient.* Knows when and how to wait until I can solve my own problem.   _____

9. *Humble.* Admits his or her own mistakes openly, learns from them, and expects subordinates to do the same.   _____

10. *Humorous.* Appreciates the lighter side of a situation. Laughs even harder when the joke is on him or her.   _____

    TOTAL   _____

Now turn the tables. Rate *yourself* as you believe your subordinates would rate you. Be honest . . . but be fair.

What can you learn from this subjective evaluation?

Managing Work

THE CLIMATE FOR SUCCESS

To work efficiently and effectively, it is helpful to have the right *climate* for success—the kind of atmosphere that concentrates everyone's attention on results, accomplishments, and achievements rather than on office politics, empire building, and petty conflict.

An organization has the right climate for success when:

- Goals and plans are clearly understood by the employees and used as the basis for everyday work.
- Necessary information moves through all levels quickly, accurately, and without bias.
- Various departments or units communicate and cooperate effectively toward achieving overall organizational objectives.
- The relationships between jobs are clear.

140

- People are encouraged to use their own initiative, feel free to question, and sense the support of higher management.
- The results expected of individuals are clearly defined, and the measures applied in judging leadership are understood.
- Its "dynamic" nature is reflected in its complete and uncomplicated planning system, innovations in its goals and decisions, and its responsiveness to change.
- Compensation is fair, competitive, and related to performance.
- Individuals see opportunities that permit development to their fullest potential.

WHAT MAKES A MOTIVATING JOB?

On July 2, 1942, Prime Minister Winston Churchill told the British House of Commons: "I am your servant, and you have the right to dismiss me when you please. What you have no right to do is ask me to bear responsibilities without the power of effective action."

People are motivated in their work by a number of things other than money or "titles." A job is usually perceived as "motivating" when it offers the following characteristics:

Enrichment

1. Skill Variety: Doing different things; using different skills, abilities, talents.

2. Task Identity: Doing a job from beginning to end, rather than doing it in bits and pieces.

3. Task Significance: The importance of the job; its "meaning."

4. Autonomy: Freedom to do the work; discretion in scheduling, decision making, and methods.

5. Feedback: Clear and direct information about job outcomes or performance.

Goals

1. Priority: Knowing and understanding the specific goals or objectives that apply to the job, plus their relative priorities.

2. Difficulty: The amount of challenge involved in reaching the goal.

Success, in the final analysis, amounts to *getting the work done.* The "sophistication" comes from doing it better, doing it faster, doing it at less cost, or doing it according to some other standard of excellence that best suits the situation.

Employees are paid to *do a job.* Whatever that job may be, whatever assistance they may have, whatever their level within the organization, they are expected to *get the work done.* Non-performance is not a standard ingredient of job security.

Here are a few suggestions that can be tried singly or in combination to help you accomplish more during your work day:

1. *Do it immediately.* Rush jobs deserve special consideration, but every job should be weighed for priority.

2. *Don't avoid unpleasant tasks.* If you avoid an unpleasant task, you carry its emotional burden with you until it's done . . . and that slows you down.

3. *Take the easiest problem first.* Handling several small tasks quickly not only gets them out of the way, it gives you some momentum and sense of accomplishment as you approach the more difficult tasks. In some situations, such as a meeting in which controversial decisions must be reached, you may establish better relations by doing away with the simpler, less debatable issues first.

4. *Do the jobs in order of their importance.* This generally is a good approach *unless* the important tasks all are very tiring or boring. This approach also may tempt you to put off or neglect certain tasks, so it should be used only if items of lower priority can be completed within a reasonable period of time.

5. *Alternate difficult tasks with easy ones.* Alternating will give you an occasional rest and something to look forward to. The variety can increase your motivation.

6. *Group similar tasks.* Doing several jobs that require the same supplies or personnel reduces duplication, provides you with better continuity, and tends to provide the most efficient utilization of your resources.

7. *Change tasks about every two hours.* Particularly when you are doing something that is routine or boring, a different type of work can relieve boredom, lift your spirits, and give you something to anticipate.

A REALISTIC PRODUCTIVITY SYSTEM

For the highly organized individual, there is a simple eight-point checklist of steps for increasing one's personal productivity:

1. List positives to be initiated.
2. List negatives to be curtailed.
3. Weigh the importance of each item.
4. Rank the difficulty of each item.
5. Match the priority and the difficulty of each item to set your priorities.
6. Use objective measures to determine the results to be expected.
7. Detail your action plan. *Who* is to do *what* and *when*?
8. Apply accountability standards for *everyone* associated with the action plan.

Using the example in Table 4-1, apply this simple method to determine where you should concentrate your personal efforts to improve productivity in your area of responsibility.

First, list the ten positive things that you should initiate and rank them in terms of importance. Then rank them in terms of difficulty. Next, determine priority by matching the important with the least difficult.

Follow the same process to determine which negative things now happening should be dealt with to achieve the greater impact on productivity.

SEVEN STEPS TO STAGNATION

Today, it seems, there must be a set of don't's to accompany every set of do's. These we will call our *Seven Steps to Stagnation*.

1. "We've never done it that way."
2. "We're not ready for that yet."
3. "We're doing all right without it."
4. "We tried it once, and it didn't work."

5. "It costs too much."

6. "That's not our responsibility."

7. "It won't work."

Table 4-1.

POSITIVE (INITIATE)			
Importance (1 most- 10 least)		*Difficulty (1 most- 10 least)*	*Priority*
9	Market share	4	
3	New accounts	9 (2)	(2)
2	Retained accounts	10 (1)	(1)
8	Sales increase	3	
1	Product development	6	
4	Customer satisfaction	7 (3)	(3)
5	Material cost	5 (4)	(4)
10	Cost of sales	1	
6	Management development	8	
7	International sourcing	2	
NEGATIVE (CURTAIL)			
Importance (1 most- 10 least)		*Difficulty (1 most- 10 least)*	*Priority*
3	Accounts receivable	10 (2)	(2)
4	Cost per unit	8 (3)	(3)
8	Customer complaints	7	
9	Product recall	2	
10	Warranty cost	3	
7	Employee benefit cost	4	
2	Absenteeism	5	
6	Energy cost	6	
1	Order turnaround	9 (1)	(1)
5	Overhead	1	

Are any of these expressions in the working vocabulary of your organization?

PLAN YOUR PROGRESS

On a sheet of paper, complete each of the following statements. Then file the paper away. In six months (mark the date on your calendar) retrieve the paper and check to see how well you have done in achieving your goals over a measured period of time.

1. My five top long-term career goals are:
2. The most important of these is:
3. The five things that will be most helpful to me in reaching my most important long-term career goal are:
4. The first task I must complete to achieve it is:
5. The five most crucial steps for the next six months are:
6. The single most important step during the next six months is:
7. The five things that will be most helpful to me in completing this step during the next six months are:
8. The first task I must complete to reach it is:

RECONCILING MANAGEMENT
PRACTICE AND THEORY

Theories about good management are all well and good—but do they *work*?

Obviously, *nothing* works of its own accord. It works if you *make* it work. Hence, the necessity to formulate a system that appeals to *you*, that suits *your own* management style and type of business, that you can implement and maintain consistently—and that you will *commit* yourself to.

Our experience is that theory and practice *can* be reconciled and *will* work productively *if* you will:

- State clear objectives.
- Hold management accountable.
- Align the interests of individuals with those of the organization.
- Show each manager the path from effective performance to the rewards he or she values.
- Reward persons who perform.
- Support creative decisions.
- Set favorable examples.

It is *results* that count. Therefore, goals should be set in the areas of greatest need. A "needs analysis," if kept simple, can be relatively easy way to focus on priorities. It is based primarily on the answers to three simple questions.

1. Where are we?
2. Where do we want to be?
3. How can we get there?

Depending on where you are, a specific goal may or may not be realistic, or a given plan of action may or may not be appropriate. It is quite normal to have differences of opinion within an organization or any or all of these questions; and until those differences are resolved, it is unlikely that the organization will accomplish much. Hence, the Needs Analysis establishes a realistic evaluation of the present situation: *Where are we now?*

To make this discovery, you must ask some basic questions about your organization or work group. You will find a format to use in the following two lists. Don't hold back. If "the enemy is within," it's probably time to say so!

Where are we now?
1. What is our basic purpose?
2. What are our strengths?
3. What are our weaknesses?
4. Are we winning or losing in: *What is the evidence*
   a. Number of percentage of those served? *Winning Losing*
      (The value of our business—sales, customers, etc.)
   b. Superiority of our service?
   c. Quality of products?
   d. Customer satisfaction?
   e. Competitive position?
   f. Productivity of our staff?
   g. Training of replacements?

What are our one-year goals?

1. What are the most important strengths or successes to be maintained?

2. What are the most important weaknesses or losses to be corrected?

    a. _____

    b. _____

    c. _____

IT'S TIME FOR A CHANGE WHEN . . .

For an organization to optimize its potential, there are certain management and organizational problems that must be met head on. According to *Supervisory Management* magazine (January 1980), it's time for a change when:

1. *We're over-structured.* Over-structuring strangles innovation, self-expression, and genuine effectiveness. An efficient, effective organization must structure itself in such a way as to best suit its unique nature, (i.e.., an organization that will maximize its strengths).

2. *We under-estimate our potential.* We need to realize what we *really* can do as people and as an organization.

3. *We wrongly compare ourselves and our competition.* Instead of making comparisons based on our potential, we are comparing our incompetencies.

4. *Our credibility is based on our image, rather than our ability or our performance.* We need methods of accountability and measurement of results. Our image always should take a back seat to our performance.

5. *We have sought and measured short-term, rather than long-term improvements.*

6. *We have a shallow level of understanding.*

7. *We try one-dimensional approaches to things.* Various disciplines should be integrated into the decision-making process.

8. *Our concepts of management are obsolete.* New ideas need to be incorporated into management at all levels.

9. *Creativity has been stifled.* We have rewarded people for conformity, good behavior, and even mediocrity. We should be rewarding creativity and risk-taking.

10. *We reinforce the wrong things.* Such things as self-expression, information-sharing, and other usually unrecognized qualities need to be reinforced.

PERFORMANCE-BASED MANAGEMENT (PBM)*

Performance-based management can lead us from where we are to where we want to be. It is a continual process by which managers periodically identify their common goals, define each individual's major area(s) of responsibility in terms of the results expected, and then use those agreed-upon measures as guide for each operating department. It also is used for assessing individual contributions to the work of the organization.

Some definitions:

1. *Objective:* The results to be accomplished. What one will have to show for the expenditure of resources and energy. Objectives must be measurable and they must be realistic, telling what will be changed, how much, when, and by whom.

2. *Goal:* Same as objective.

3. *Mission:* A never-ending, ongoing reason for being. Something for which we constantly strive, but will never completely achieve.

4. *Purpose:* Same as mission.

5. *Key Result Area:* A designation or category of responsibilities for which we must find a way to measure. Ask yourself: What am I accountable for (customer service, sales volume, production levels, profits, quality control, or personnel development). These should be identified *before* we try to measure accomplishments.

6. *Success Indicator:* A way to measure change. Tells *how* to measure accomplishments. The four broad categories of indicator are quantity, quality, time, and cost.

7. *Activity:* An expenditure of energy, a program, something one *does* as opposed to someting one *makes happen* (creates). A means, as opposed to an end.

*Copyright 1981 Roger Fritz & Associates.

8. *Input:* An asset, a resource, something needed to do work. A tool, not an end.

9. *Output:* What we accomplished. The outcome of productive effort. The value added by a wise selection among alternatives, and the additional benefits enjoyed due to the timely and energetic expenditure of effort and resources.

Performance-Based Management: Conditions for Success

Does performance-based management meet everyone's needs? Can it be quickly and easily instituted in an organization? In a word, no.

In order for performance-based management to be successful, an organization needs:

- An environment for change.
- A Chief Executive who is committed to the concept.
- Development of the Chief Executive's own objectives.
- A rigid timetable for installation.
- Results orientation within the organization.
- A complete systematic installation.

Benefits from Performance-Based Management

Under this concept, people make commitments in a goal-setting session and then have a charter to go ahead with their work under self-control. Managers have more freedom to do their jobs without interference from above—no second-guessing, no looking over the shoulder, no breathing down the neck, and no requests for explanations after every action.

People get an opportunity to set objectives for their own jobs. This is not carte blanche, but it does mean that the individual manager has a chance to sell his or her own concept of the purpose of the job. Even if he or she fails to sell the idea, he or she still has the satisfaction of having been heard.

People are aware of the performance that is sought and of what they are being rewarded (or penalized) for. Commitments

149

are made "up front." People get rewarded for successfully achieving their objectives. The risk of failure still is present, but the people know—in advance—what is expected of them.

Performance-based management affords more people more participation than they usually enjoy in an organization where the orders flow from the top down and the reports flow from the bottom up. The concept also is a marked improvement over traditional, intuitive management systems in which people do not know what is expected of them in advance but are rewarded or punished according to standards that are invented after the fact.

Performance-based management affords powerful and significant benefits to employees which, behavioral research shows, meet the needs of an increasing number of managers in today's work force.

Performance-Based Management: Requirements at the Top

As previously stated, performance-based management requires that the Chief Executive be committed to the concept and that, as George Odiorne points out, this requires a number of other commitments. The Chief Executive must:

1. Set an example and not merely order his or her people to practice the concept or talk favorably about it.

2. Assign responsibility for liaison work in implementing the system to a person who has the backing and support of the line managers who will be executing it.

3. Be willing to dig into details whenever the system seems to be faltering and to direct whatever changes are needed to get it back on track.

4. Be willing to listen to complaints about the system but insist that it continue to be used.

5. Praise and reward the people who make the system succeed. The criticism of heel draggers, critics, cynics, and saboteurs must be dealt with privately, one-on-one.

6. Become a student of the concept and its related management practices. This means keeping up with new ideas, trends, and applications (e.g., quality circles) and reporting on them to the organization.

7. Weigh and publicize the payoffs and gains regularly. If something is working, encourage more of it; if something isn't, change it or eliminate it.

Executives and managers must:

1. Continuously innovate and change the system for the better. Tying the concept to suggestion awards, organization development, and special programs like productivity, quality control and other real-life concerns will give the program the vitality it needs to stay alive and healthy.
2. Develop a method of checking and correcting the system, seeing how it is going and keeping it on course.
3. Be willing to take some risks. If you have a dangerous safety problem, hang the solution on this system. If you need an improvement in productivity, make that one of the major objectives of the system.
4. Show confidence and optimism. A leader who expresses doubt and cynicism, or who downgrades the efforts that are made, will destroy the performance-based management concepts.

GUIDES TO ACTION

The introduction of a new management concept, such as performance-based management, requires a great deal of commitment; but these nine guidelines will make the implementation a great deal easier:

1. Introduce the system from the top down.
2. Recognize that the participation of subordinates will depend upon the climate of the organization.
3. The most favorable results will stem from the greatest participation.
4. Begin by establishing clear goals for the program itself, and then follow through with extensive training.
5. Provide feedback regarding the system's performance at frequent intervals.
6. Remember that the best feedback is supportive and helpful, not judgmental.
7. The performance-based management concept cannot succeed without the support of all supervisors.
8. Performance-based management cannot succeed without organizational support.

9. Regular monitoring of the system involves checks on attitude, relationships, *and* performance.

"PROFILING" YOUR ORGANIZATION DEVELOPMENT

Bear in mind, once again, the three basic questions involved in a performance-based management system: Where are we? Where do we want to be? How do we get there?

With these questions in mind, develop a "profile" of your plan by studying these questions:

1. What business are we in?
2. What business should we be in, the next five years?
3. What are the products/services of our organization (unit, section, division, group)?
4. What are the key result areas of my job? What are the success indicators?

Key result examples	*Success indicator examples*
Negotiating settlements	Agreements reached before deadline
Processing orders	Time per order
Machine maintenance	Downtime
Customer/client contact	Retained or new customers/clients
Selling	Product/service sales volume/profit

5. On what basis do I judge my subordinates' performance?
6. On what basis does (should) my manager judge my performance?
7. What is my responsibility in developing personnel?
8. If I were promoted, who would take my position? Is he or she ready now? If not, what is needed and how long should it take?
9. What type of training is needed to achieve the results I (we) must obtain?
10. What is my contribution to profits and control of expenses?
11. What changes are needed in my department in the next three months, six months, twelve months?
12. What things are needed for my own personal development in order for me to be successful?

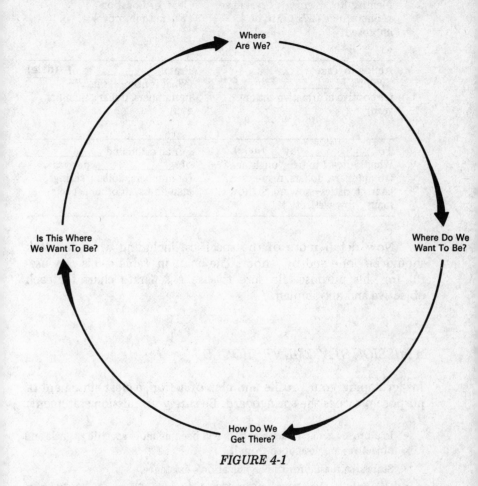

FIGURE 4-1

HOW TO STATE AN OBJECTIVE

As you write down your objectives, follow the format in Table 4-2. Use the same form in stating your objectives in each key result area.

Table 4-2.

Identify Key Element: Crystallize & Summarize (*What* is to be improved)	Dept. or Location (Where to improve)
Action to Take "Will be_____" (A positive affirmative action verb)	From _____ as of _(date)_ (What is now—*"isness"*— In numbers, dollars, man-hrs, etc.)
To _____ by _(date)_ What is *ought* to be—"oughtness"— (to numbers, dollars, man-hours, characteristics—how much, how many, how well, etc.)	For an estimated _____ of _____ per year (in numbers, dollars, savings, man-hours, or other aspects)

Now detail more of the specifics, including when the task should be done and by whom. The chart in Table 4-3 is very useful for this purpose. Be sure to use a separate chart for each objective and action plan.

A MISSION STATEMENT SHOULD . . .

In developing your profile and plan of action, a clear statement of purpose provides the springboard. Be sure your mission statement:

- Is a broad, general statement. It will become more specific as goals and objectives are developed from it.
- States the reason for the organization's existence.
- Commits to specific purposes, which in turn will govern specific programs.
- Includes restrictions (for example, if the decision has been made to exclude a specific service).
- Is formulated at the Board of Directors' level.
- Is in writing.
- Is widely disseminated.

Preparation of an agreement on the overall mission of the organization is followed by the determination of long-range goals. These lead to more specific objectives within an annual time frame, which then are interpreted at the unit level, as illustrated by the diagram in Figure 4-2.

THE EIGHT BASICS

As an individual, there are some things that you should do as a part of the performance-based management process:

1. Define your key result areas.
2. Determine how to measure success in each area.
3. Take stock of your present performance in each area, using the measurement indicators chosen.
4. Prepare a draft stating the level of performance to which you are ready to commit yourself.
5. Negotiate all of the above with your immediate administrative superior.
6. Monitor progress as the weeks go by.
7. Review performance with your superior at least once each quarter.
8. Summarize the year's results in a review with your superior as the basis for starting the cycle over again the following year.

THE CONCEPT OF KEY RESULT AREAS

Activity is not the same as results, and *results* are what we're after.
What is a key result area?
A prevailing attitude among many people who hesitate or refuse to commit themselves to objectives is the belief that "You can't measure my work." You hear this especially from those who deal with intangibles, with values and with services, as opposed to those whose jobs involve more visible results, such as manufactured items, dollars, or buildings.

Table 4-3 OBJECTIVES & PLANS OF ACTION

Dept: BUSINESS OFFICE
Position: SUPERVISOR
Prepared by:
Date: 2-2-
Page 1 of 1 Pages

OBJECTIVES & RESULTS *SPECIFIC RESULTS* to be accomplished: WHAT WHEN WHERE and NET COST-BENEFIT	PLAN OF ACTION Sequenced, step-by-step action to take: HOW TO ACCOMPLISH IT	When to Be Done (Schedule)	Who is to Do it (Assgnm't)	"Pin the Rose" Auth. 1/ to Act (Delegt'n)	Comm. with Whom	Status & Dates
Objective #1 of 5 Weight 25%						
A microfiche system for out-patient itemized bills and zero bills—in the business office to eliminate preparation, matching, in-filing, out-filing, and microfiming of 4000 out-patients p/month will be put into effect by 2-14-	1. Realign out-patient registration procedures.		R.S. S.S.			
	A. *Prepare procedures and flow charts*—covering the new self-pay system.	2-4	R.S. S.S.	A	C.Z. W.B.	
	B. *Train out-registration clerks* to phase out the preparation of self-pay folders and to put new system of self pay folders into effect.	2-7	S.S.	A	R.S.	
—for a reduction in lost time accounts, retrieval time, filing space and errors	C. *Discontinue preparation of self-pay out-patient folders*—in out-patient registration department.	2-7	S.S.	A	R.S.	
—with estimated savings of $30,000 p/year	D. *Maintain a file of registration forms*—by dates and deliver to out-patient supervisor.	2-7	S.S.	A	R.S.	

2. Realign the file room procedures.

A. *Prepare procedures and flow charts*—covering the file room procedures.	2-10	L.A. R.S.	A	C.Z. W.B.
B. *Train file room staff*—in microfiche systems and procedures.	2-10	L.A.	A	R.S.
C. *Check self-pay bills*—for accuracy and completeness.	2-10	L.A.	A	R.S.
D. *Maintain a file of self-pay bills*—and deliver to supervisor.	2-10	L.A.	A	R.S.
E. *Preparation of self-pay room folders.*	2-14	L.A.	A	R.S.

Distribution to:

Reviewed by:	Position:	Dates:	Follow-up:

GOALS AT EACH LEVEL

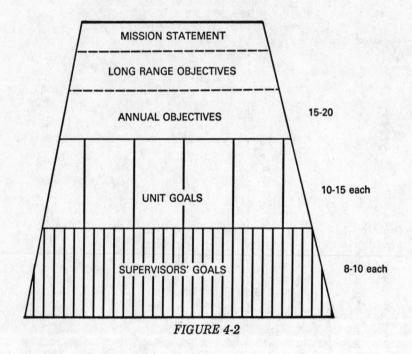

FIGURE 4-2

Certainly, it is more difficult to measure the results of some jobs than of others, but it is not impossible. Indeed, it is very difficult to measure *any* job in its *entirety*; therefore, we should not try to measure the whole job, but should break that job down into its component parts.

Itemize the separate responsibilities or duties which the job entails, and call these discrete parts of the job Key Result Areas. They are not goals, but they are areas of concern which we will turn into goals. They will become goals when we determine how to measure them and add a precise level of accomplishment (or change).

A key result area, then, answers the questions: What am I trying to measure? What are the things I am accountable for? What are the major components of my job?

There are three basic phases involved in the implementation of a performance-based management system.

Phase one: Thinking about *the system.* You're really not committed to the system yet. The old system is "comfortable." Performance-based management appeals to you because it is *logical.*

Phase two: Thinking into *the system.* You have chosen to act and have acquired some experience in implementing new programs. You're now thinking operationally about the system and about how-to-do-it concerns, such as what kinds of training to propose, what the course should include, who should teach it, what forms might be used, and how widespread the program should be. Key problems are timing and how to "sell" the idea in the organization. You're afraid of making a mistake that will defeat the concept before it even gets started. You're probably shaping your program plan and choosing people who will be responsible for implementing the system.

Phase three: Thinking through *the system.* You are in an organization that follows performance-based management concepts and you have worked with the system for a few years, experiencing some successes and some failures. Due to the successes, you suspect that you would have real trouble abandoning the concept now, but there still are some problems to be resolved: How do you apply the concept to staff jobs, such as legal, accounting, personnel? How can you tell if people really are doing a job of coaching or mindlessly following the performance review procedures? How should your performance appraisal system operate? How do you identify high-potential people? How do merit raises fit into the system? Should you be trying selection by objectives?

When performance-based management has truly become a *system of management*, rather than a *concept*, all of these issues and more are common. This is when you're really thinking *through* the system.

ORGANIZATION BENEFITS
FROM PERFORMANCE-BASED MANAGEMENT

Obviously, it's easier to remain with something "comfortable" than to change to something new. If you are to adopt performance-based management, it should offer the organization a number of marked benefits.

Here are a few good reasons for making the change:

- We're making these decisions anyway. The challenge is to make them *better.*
- Discriminatory judgment must be made *in favor* of excellence.
- Management development begins with a system to insure regular communication between bosses and subordinates based on performance.
- The end results are specific, but the ways of getting there are left open.
- By checking and defining areas of responsibility, we get at the source of future problems and take steps to correct them, rather than trying to trace blame.
- The stigma of poor performance tends to remain longer when appraisals are informal and unwritten than when they are formalized and recorded over a period of time.
- The faintest ink is better than the finest memory.
- By reviewing and recording their views, both supervisor and subordinate have a better opportunity to face up to their difference. It will be more difficult to hide incompetence in either person.
- Without objectives, you never will be able to see what you did or did not achieve.

THE PERFORMANCE-BASED MANAGEMENT "CYCLE"

Different types of organizations will approach performance-based management from different perspectives. A business organization is not like an educational institution or a health care institution, although all are excellent candidates for such an approach to management.

Whatever the nature of the organization, the functions of performance-based management can be illustrated in a cycle. (See Figures 4-3 through 4-6.)

STEPS FOR INSTALLING THE SYSTEM

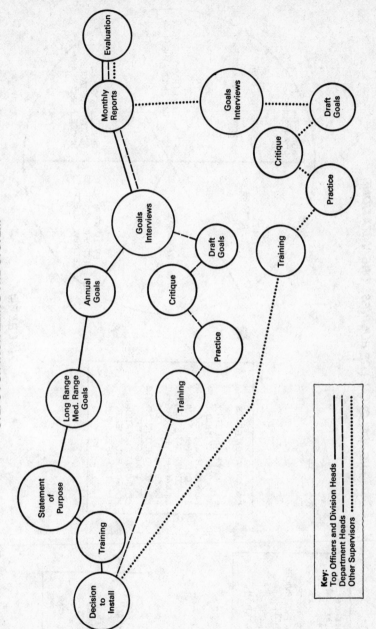

Key:
Top Officers and Division Heads ──────
Department Heads ── ── ──
Other Supervisors ·········

FIGURE 4-3

THE PBM CYCLE FOR BUSINESS ORGANIZATIONS

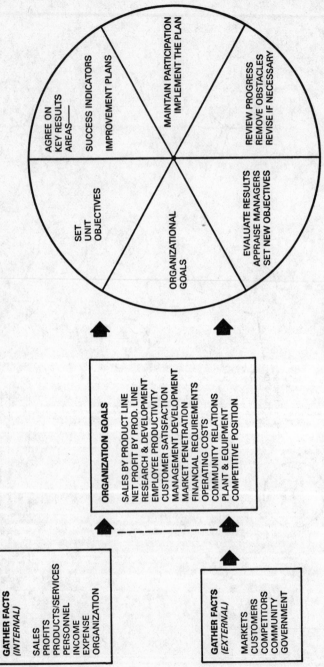

GATHER FACTS *(INTERNAL)*

SALES
PROFITS
PRODUCTS/SERVICES
PERSONNEL
INCOME
EXPENSE
ORGANIZATION

ORGANIZATION GOALS

SALES BY PRODUCT LINE
NET PROFIT BY PROD. LINE
RESEARCH & DEVELOPMENT
EMPLOYEE PRODUCTIVITY
CUSTOMER SATISFACTION
MANAGEMENT DEVELOPMENT
MARKET PENETRATION
FINANCIAL REQUIREMENTS
OPERATING COSTS
COMMUNITY RELATIONS
PLANT & EQUIPMENT
COMPETITIVE POSITION

GATHER FACTS *(EXTERNAL)*

MARKETS
CUSTOMERS
COMPETITORS
COMMUNITY
GOVERNMENT

AGREE ON
KEY RESULTS
AREAS
SUCCESS INDICATORS
IMPROVEMENT PLANS

MAINTAIN PARTICIPATION
IMPLEMENT THE PLAN

REVIEW PROGRESS
REMOVE OBSTACLES
REVISE IF NECESSARY

SET
UNIT
OBJECTIVES

ORGANIZATIONAL
GOALS

EVALUATE RESULTS
APPRAISE MANAGERS
SET NEW OBJECTIVES

FIGURE 4-4

THE PBM CYCLE FOR EDUCATION INSTITUTIONS

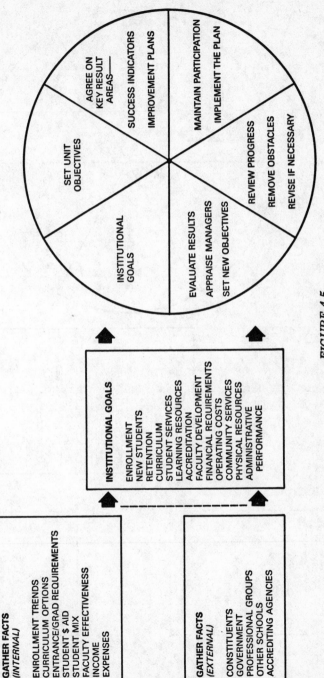

GATHER FACTS
(INTERNAL)

ENROLLMENT TRENDS
CURRICULUM OPTIONS
ENTRANCE/GRAD REQUIREMENTS
STUDENT $ AID
STUDENT MIX
FACULTY EFFECTIVENESS
INCOME
EXPENSES

GATHER FACTS
(EXTERNAL)

CONSTITUENTS
GOVERNMENT
PROFESSIONAL GROUPS
OTHER SCHOOLS
ACCREDITING AGENCIES

INSTITUTIONAL GOALS

ENROLLMENT
NEW STUDENTS
RETENTION
CURRICULUM
STUDENT SERVICES
LEARNING RESOURCES
ACCREDITATION
FACULTY DEVELOPMENT
FINANCIAL REQUIREMENTS
OPERATING COSTS
COMMUNITY SERVICES
PHYSICAL RESOURCES
ADMINISTRATIVE
PERFORMANCE

INSTITUTIONAL
GOALS

SET UNIT
OBJECTIVES

AGREE ON
KEY RESULT
AREAS

SUCCESS INDICATORS
IMPROVEMENT PLANS

MAINTAIN PARTICIPATION
IMPLEMENT THE PLAN

REVIEW PROGRESS
REMOVE OBSTACLES
REVISE IF NECESSARY

EVALUATE RESULTS
APPRAISE MANAGERS
SET NEW OBJECTIVES

FIGURE 4-5

THE PBM CYCLE FOR HEALTH CARE INSTITUTIONS

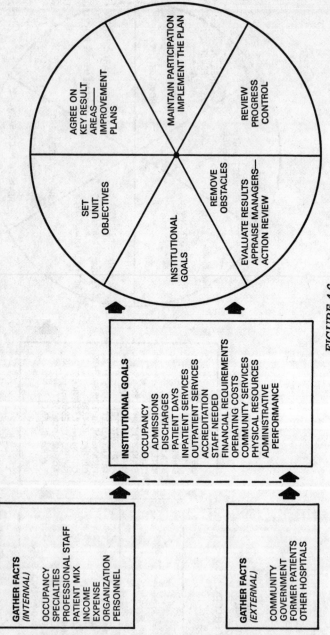

FIGURE 4-6

EMPLOYEE ADVANTAGES
IN PERFORMANCE-BASED MANAGEMENT

Performance-based management benefits the employee as much as it does the organization.

For *supervisors* and *managers*, it is:

- A basis for continuing communication.
- A way to better interpersonal relationships based on performance factors.
- A basis for increased options toward motivating subordinates.
- A means to a more accurate appraisal.
- A pathway to improved results.

For *subordinates*, performance-based management is:

- A clarification of authority and accountability.
- A chance to participate in the process of setting goals and performance standards.
- A means of knowing what results are expected.
- A way to relate personal satisfaction (or lack of it) to job performance.
- A way to assure regular feedback.

TWELVE WAYS TO MAKE IT WORK

As we stated once before, performance-base management will not work unless you *make* it work. No other system will, either.

If you *want* the benefits of performance-based management, if you *want* the increased freedom and efficiency it affords, if you *want* to succeed and be instrumental in helping your personnel to succeed, here are some ways in which to *make* the system work:

1. Plan your program carefully.
2. Prepare the participants through training.
3. Provide some guidelines for people to follow in setting their own goals.
4. Make sure that the network of goals is understood.

5. Realize that the achievement of goals isn't always directly related to performance. Luck can play a part.

6. Don't think of goals only in a narrow, single-year time frame; think of multiyear goals, too.

7. Hire a performance-based management administrator and make him or her responsible for overseeing the system.

8. Allow the system to be flexible, and don't make conformity a goal.

9. Don't tie goals directly to compensation.

10. Keep the system simple, especially in the start-up phase.

11. Communicate top management's goals throughout the organization.

12. Treat the concept as a system of managing, not as an addition to people's jobs or as the "pet" of some staff department.

IF THERE'S FAINT ENTHUSIASM . . .

Nothing new is every received with total enthusiasm by *all* of the people involved, but in time, a few "successes" will make believers out of anyone.

When performance-based management has been implemented, when it has had a period of time in which to "prove" itself, and there are those who *still* lack enthusiasm for it, the reason probably stems from one of the following:

1. Lack of commitment to the concept by the Chief Executive and/or others in top management.

2. Autocratic behavior by the Chief Executive during implementation ("We're going to have measurable objectives around here. Here are the ones I have worked out for you!")

3. Failure to negotiate on performance range indicators between bosses and their subordinates.

4. Assignment of full responsibility for the implementation to staff functions (usually Personnel or Controller) or to an "Assistant to" without any further commitment by top management.

5. An assumption by top management that performance-based management is primarily a tool for training managers, not a framework for

decision making and problem solving, or a complete management system.

6. Resistance at lower management levels because it has been perceived by them as "another paper work project."

7. Fear at lower management levels that the system will jeopardize existing management information systems or not be compatible with existing operational data.

8. Fear by employees that the system is a disguised performance-review technique.

9. The assumption that budgeting and financial controls are identical or tantamount to performance-based management.

10. The assumption that the concept is something radically new and untested.

11. The assumption that performance-based management can be introduced with minimal effort and within a short time frame.

12. The introduction of the system at middle management levels without support by top management.

13. The assumption by the Chief Executive that, although the system is fine for subordinates, his or her objectives could not be reduced to writing, nor could his or her performance be evaluated in this manner.

14. The assumption by staff personnel that their work is impossible to measure.

WHEN PERFORMANCE-BASED MANAGEMENT DOESN'T WORK . . .

. . . the chances are, it's because:

- Management isn't committed.
- Goals aren't set participatively.
- Supervisors aren't well trained.
- Feedback is missing.
- Reviews aren't conducted regularly.
- The link between the system and compensation is poor.

Success with performance-based management is not guaranteed. Success never is.

Though not difficult to understand, performance-based management requires perseverance. Significant benefits often do not accrue for three to five years.

Proficiency with the system takes *continuous* learning and reinforcement.

Managers must differentiate between activities and results, between efficiency and effectiveness, between busyness and accomplishment.

Some people prefer not to press for participative management and are more successful as authoritarians. If avoided, the negotiation of goals in jointly held areas of responsibility will cause the system to fail.

Restrictions

1. Benefits of performance-based management are lost if the system is viewed as a means of "tightening the screws" to get more production, without regard for the employees.

2. The paper work can become burdensome and unjustified, unless goals and success indicators are carefully prepared and limited in number.

3. Training is needed continuously to help people cope with new situations.

4. Performance based on goals should be appraised continuously, not just at the officially designated intervals.

Restraints

1. Supervisors must initiate action. Little happens unless they do.

2. Performance-based management requires joint goal setting, agreement on key results expected, and agreement on the measures of progress.

3. Emphasis is on the "what" more than the "how." For many experienced managers, this is a difficult discipline.

4. Performance-based management stresses negotiation "up front" and commitment when risks are greater because less is known.

PERFORMANCE-BASED MANAGEMENT FIGHTS INERTIA

Performance-based management combats management inertia that can exist when:

- Planning and goals are not well understood.
- Jobs are not defined in terms of key results.
- Continued learning of management skills and self-development is limited.
- Decision making is not delegated and decentralized.
- Accountability is unclear.
- Information is lacking for effective problem solving.

TEN CALENDAR EVENTS

If your organization is oriented to performance-based management, it is helpful to prepare a calendar listing key dates for which certain actions should be targeted. This makes the system of managing by objectives coherent and helps disperse the system throughout the entire organization.

Event one: Closing date for filing rolling five-year plans for the organization and its major units should be six months before the beginning of the measurement year. The annual edition of the five-year plan should well up from all major staff departments and profit centers.

Event two: Budgets should be submitted three months in advance of the measurement year. They should include all resources movements, additions, and requests, and should reflect anything that showed up in the five-year plan as it affects the next year's budget.

Event three: Every manager should start issuing appointments for goal setting and performance review during the last month of the program year.

Event four: Every manager and subordinate should meet during the first month of the new program year to discuss objectives for the coming year and results for the previous year. These discussions should be related to long-range planning, to budget commitments, and to the subordinate's commitments for the coming year. Confirm each discussion with a memo.

Event five: The boss should complete the annual report for each subordinate's personnel folder during the first month of the new year. The report should describe the subordinate's objectives and achievements for the year just ended.

Event six: The management committee should review the results of the entire organization each month. Reviews of special problem areas also should be conducted monthly.

Event seven: The boss should meet with each subordinate at the end of each quarter to review the annual goals of the subordinate and make adjustments as needed.

Event eight: For supervisory management, salary reviews should be conducted on the anniversary dates of their employment. For middle and upper management, they should be conducted at longer intervals—up to thirty-six months for certain key officers.

Event nine: Audits of all financial data and program audits in other areas should be conducted and completed during the first quarter of the new year. These audits should then be used in preparing the next edition of the five-year plan.

Event ten: Assessments of promotability should be made through annual review board meetings of the top managers of the organization, producing a statement of the personal growth and development of high-talent people in the organization.

HOW TO AUDIT THE SYSTEM

Yes, the performance-based management system should be audited, and the process will be a lot smoother and more productive if you will review these suggestions and questions:

1. Along with the insiders on your audit team, make use of some outside advisors who have had experience with a number of other organizations.

2. Use only top-level people for the audit, not lower-level technicians. When the final recommendations come out, they must have considerable credibility if they are to be converted into action.

3. The review should include the study of all the actual statements of objectives that have been prepared in the normal course of operations.

4. Are there gaps in the expectations of a boss and his or her subordinate?

5. Are people talking face to face to determine goals and criteria, or do they simply exchange memos?

6. Are the goals statements focused on the few vital things that need doing?

7. Have you allowed enough time for the system to take hold and succeed, or have you been betting on a "quick fix"?

8. Has your implementation been orderly, starting with a clear diagnosis of the present management method, followed by thorough instruction in the new approach, its philosophy, and its techniques? Do you have a systematic way of dealing with problems?

9. Who is responsible for making the system work? This can be a steering committee to help the system gain acceptance, or it can be the function of a responsible administrator.

GOALS ON YOUR JOB

As a manager, some of your time is spent on repetitive, routine, regular, recurring bread-and-butter operational concerns. These are the normal work output of you and your group. Objectives covering these responsibilities are called *routine* objectives.

Part of your time is spent solving problems. When you are results-oriented, problems concern not only the unpleasantnesses, obstacles, and interruptions on the job, but outputs with which you are not satisfied. Problems concern those key result areas in which performance is currently not meeting a satisfactory norm.

Still another part of your time is spent on developmental, innovative areas—things you are doing because of their long-term impact on your operation. They deal with change, which could mean some new project you're getting into for the first time, some new way of doing an old project, or some unique, one-shot program. You are engaged in them, however, because they add to the results produced by you and your group. We call these *innovative* objectives, and they are the exact opposite of the routine or repetitive objectives.

There is a managment theory that, as a manager moves from one type of goal to another, he or she climbs the ladder of excellence. A manager who simply takes care of routine areas of responsibility has the repetitive things under control and runs a tight ship, which is valued within an organization. Worth more, however, is the manager who isn't flustered when things go a little out of control, who actually expects this occasionally, and who is wise in finding ways to solve problems as they arise.

Worth even more is the individual who not only controls routine affairs *and* solves problems when they arise (both of which are problems of the present), but who can look to the future. This is the person who is developmental, innovative, and creative.

Where is the *fun* in managing? In the control of routine, repetitive work? Of course not. The challenge is in the area of innovation—problem solving. *But*—one cannot work with future situations and innovations until the routine matters are under control. Therefore, start with the routine, define acceptable standards for them *first*, get them under control, and *then* you can delegate them to someone else while you turn your attention to innovation and problem solving.

Why bother to set goals for the routine tasks?

Because you do not want your people to be devoting all of their time and energy to the "new" and the "glamorous," the "exciting," and the "frills." Someone must watch the day-to-day operations.

A *total* list of job-related goals must include the routine as well as the "thrilling." (See Table 4-4.)

Categories and Classes of Goals

An anonymous individual once said (or wrote): "If you can't see where you're going, you may not like where you end up."

Hannah More added: "Obstacles are those frightful things you see when you take your eyes off the goal."

There are two main types of goals: personal goals and job-related goals. The wise manager determines what his or her goals

Table 4-4. HOW TO THINK ABOUT JOB-RELATED GOALS

MISSION/ROLE	ORGANIZATIONAL POSITION	JOB DESCRIPTION
	KEY RESULT AREAS	*Which Are Either*
Routine	Problem	Innovative
What is your group's normal work output?	What are the norms for your group's work output?	What new ideas does your group plan to work on?
What are the measurable units or aspects for each output?	In which areas is performance currently not up to these standards?	What will be the measurable added benefits?
How many units of this output will be required this period?	How much measurable improvement is realistic this period?	What will be the costs to generate these benefits?
Consider using a range to describe the outputs.	What action steps will be taken to remedy the situation?	What steps can be monitored as time goes by?

are *in both categories*, because *success* and *happiness* are not synonymous—and the latter requires a careful blending of the two.

	Job-related goals	
Classes	*What it concerns*	*Type of commitment*
Routine	Normal work output	Meeting standards
Problem-solving	Results below par	Finding a solution
Innovative	Something new	Seeking added benefits

	Personal development	
Classes	*What it concerns*	*Type of commitment*
Technical/Professional growth	Information, skills,	Effort to meet a need
Managerial development	Information, skills, attitudes	Effort to meet a need
Growth as a person	Information, skills, attitudes	Effort to meet a need

Short-Term Individual Goals

While managing the work of the organization, it is important to keep your short-term *individual* goals in mind. These should:

- Flow from the position description.
- Be consistent with, and take their cue from, overall organization goals.
- Be measurable—a requirement that necessitates the development of suitable standards and yardsticks.
- Be challenging, in order to provide motivation and a feeling of real accomplishment.
- Be attainable and reasonably within the control of the individual.
- Initially, be limited. After a time, managers will learn to handle a greater number of goals effectively.
- Be arranged in priority so that, when difficulties arises regarding alternative courses of action, decisions can be made according to their proper level of importance.

What Is a Workable Goal?

A goal is not worthwhile if it is not practical, workable, attainable. If a goal is to be workable, it should:

1. Be negotiated up, down, and across the organizational spectrum.
2. Be one of a limited number. Confine yourself to five or six.
3. Support overall organization objectives.
4. Be a guide to action, stating "what," not "how."
5. Be explicit and measurable.
6. Offer a challenge, so that the achievement is significant.
7. Be designed in view of the factors which are not controlled by the person involved, such as budget limitations.
8. Motivate people to want to achieve them.
9. Be reviewed periodically.
10. Provide the basis for a performance appraisal.

THE MOST COMMON ERRORS IN GOAL-SETTING

Setting goals incorrectly or setting the *wrong* goals can be as much of a turn-*off* as a turn-*on*.

174

Here are some of the common errors that are made in setting goals. Avoid them at all costs.

1. The manager fails to clarify common objectives for *the whole unit.*
2. Goals are set so low they do not challenge the individual subordinate.
3. Prior results are not used as a basis for finding new and unusual combinations.
4. The unit's common objectives are not blended with those of the larger unit of which it is a part.
5. Individuals are overloaded with inappropriate or impossible goals.
6. Responsibilities are not clustered in the most appropriate positions.
7. Two or more individuals are allowed to believe themselves responsible for doing exactly the same thing.
8. Methods (the "how") are stressed, rather than clarifying individual areas of responsibility (the "what").
9. Emphasis is placed on pleasing the boss, rather than achieving the job objective.
10. No policies are set as guides to action. The boss waits for results, *then* issues ad hoc judgments by means of correction.
11. No probing is done to discover what the subordinate's program for goal achievement will be. Every goal is accepted uncritically, without a plan for its successful achievement.
12. The boss is too reluctant to add his or her own (or higher management's) known needs to the subordinates' programs.
13. Real obstacles are ignored, including allowances for many emergency or routine duties which will consume time.
14. Subordinates' new goals or ideas are ignored, and the boss imposes only those which he or she wants.
15. The boss doesn't think through and act upon the things he or she must do to help the subordinate succeed.
16. Intermediate target dates (milestones) by which to measure progress are not set.
17. No new ideas are introduced from outside the organization, thereby freezing the status quo.
18. New goals are not allowed to supplant stated objectives that are of less importance.
19. Previously agreed-upon goals have not been discarded, even though proven to be unfeasible, irrelevant, or impossible.

20. Successful behavior has not been reinforced after a goal has been achieved.

DO YOUR GOALS MATCH THE RUMBA?

A good goal must be effective. Lest you forget that when negotiating goals with your supervisor—or subordinates—see if the proposed goal is equal to the RUMBA, which simply means that an effective goal is:

- *R*elevant: It meets highest priority needs.
- *U*nderstandable: Clearly and concisely written.
- *M*easurable: Success indicators are negotiated.
- *B*ehavioral: The people involved are committed.
- *A*chievable: It can be done.

DEFINING ROUTINE OBJECTIVES

For more specific guidance in defining routine objectives, these pointers may help:

1. The first step is to outline the "structure" that reports to you—prepare a rough organization chart. The titles of subordinates usually are a general indicator of areas of responsibility that you hold.
2. Using the chart and your own job description, list your major result areas.
3. If you or your subordinates have commitments to other programs, they should be stated in terms of output (results).
4. Check objectives at a higher level to make sure yours are in tune.
5. Equate your results with outputs or end results. Don't mix inputs or activities, such as money and programs, with them.
6. The effects you are seeking should be things you hope to make happen, and should include the significant areas in which you would like your performance to be measured and judged. Results stated should be attainable.

7. It sometimes helps to list two or three things you made happen on your job within the last six months. From them, you can project other things you *expect* to make happen during the next quarter, six months, or year.

8. Make sure that your job encompasses the results you are seeking.

9. In staff areas, remember that the *program* goes before the *budget*. "Performance budgeting" is not simply spending last year's budget plus 10 percent. It is defining what *should* be done, determining what it is likely to cost, gaining budgetary approval, and then administering both program and budget effectively.

10. For each of the major areas you list:
    a. What is the lowest permissible (acceptable) level of achievement (i.e., the level below which you would be in trouble)? Using the type of planning chart shown in Table 4-5, list this level under "minimum acceptable."
    b. If you had to bet on a probable outcome, what would it be? What do you expect to be the average for next year? Show this under "expected average" on the chart.
    c. What is the best level you can reasonably expect? Show this as the "maximum probable."

11. Do you see any trade-offs between major result areas? Remembering that the volume of work is affected by the quality that is expected, do you want to reverse any of the levels of performance, based on the trade-offs you have identified?

The chart in Table 4-6 shows some sample routine objectives. You should prepare your own objectives using the worksheet in Table 4-5.

EXPRESSING GOALS

An organization's goals depend on the type of work for which it is responsible. Therefore, a goal may be expressed in terms of:

Raw data

1. The number of cases handled per quarter
2. 7 promotable managers
3. Units produced per shift

Table 4-5. ROUTINE GOALS WORKSHEET

List here your regular, routine (job description) kind of objectives. Refer to your position description. List in left-hand column the results areas that are most critical in your job this year. Incude the "trade-off" objectives; for example, the volume of work will be influenced by the quality expected.

KEY RESULT AREAS	INDICATORS (QUALITY, QUANTITY, TIME, COST)	PRESENT LEVEL	RESULTS USING INDICATORS CHOSEN		
			Minimum Acceptable	*Expected Average*	*Maximum Probable*

Table 4-6. SAMPLE ROUTINE OBJECTIVES

Key Result Area	As Measured By	Present Level	DESIRED LEVEL		
			Min.	Aver.	Max.
Budget Administration	1. Variance	1%	3%	2%	0%
Revenue	1. Gross income per year	$3,125,600	3.4	3.6	3.75
Productivity of Work Force	1. Number units per man-hour	10	10	12	14
	2. Cost of service per man-hour	8.74	9.70	9.34	8.92
Cost Control	1. Additional cost increase	4%	3%	1%	0
Payments	1. Number accounts paid before first of month	75%	85%	95%	98%
	2. Decreased number of deferred payments	150	100	75	50
PBM Management System	1. Number of one-to-one superior/subordinate evaluations	—	3	4	6
	2. Number of clarified job descriptions	—	18/21	21/21	21/21
	3. Percent Dept. goals in target results	—	75%	85%	95%
	4. Procedure manual	—	verbal	written	manual
Affirmative Action	1. Number of minority:				
	a. department managers	1	3	4	5
	b. salesmen	2	2	3	4
	c. foreman	5	6	8	9
	d. office supervisors	1	3	5	7
	e. secretaries	43	50	60	70
General Appearance and Condition	1. Number of interrupted schedules due to carelessness	3 per week	2	1	0
	2. Number of chargeable incidents	4 per week	3	2	1
	3. Number of inventory forms indicating repairs, etc.	30 per quarter	15	10	5

4. 7,200 paid subscribers
5. 180 returns

Ratios

1. 90 percent on-time departures
2. 10 percent over or under budget
3. 35 percent share of market
4. 92 percent rehabilitation rate
5. Downtime as a percentage of total running time

Scales

1. Temperatures
2. Weights
3. Ratings on a scale of 1-10, 1-100, etc.

CONDUCTING A GOAL-SETTING SESSION

To make the performance-based management process work most effectively, the goal-setting discussion should be heightened in significance by being made a conscious, formal, and scheduled interview. This means that the boss should not only schedule the interviews but should issue a written list of them to go out to all affected people.

This should be followed by some specific plans for making the whole discussion process work better, such as:

- Holding a staff meeting to announce the schedule and to give some instructions on what information should be brought to the goal-setting interview. This improves the quality of the goals that subordinates propose.
- Announcing any assumptions or prior conditions *in advance*.
- Suggesting that subordinates bring their own agendas of points to be covered during the goal-setting discussion, along with any back-up documentation that might be helpful.
- Preparing a similar set of notes, documentation, and expectations in preparation for the goal-setting discussion with each subordinate manager.

- Arranging for a private discussion—uninterrupted by phone calls or drop-ins, and setting aside all other matters during the discussion.

- Providing a relaxed atmosphere for the goal-setting discussion. For example, the boss should not sit behind a desk, grilling the subordinate, but should sit on the same side of the table with the subordinate.

- Insisting on improvement goals and innovations. The boss also should show support for the ideas of the subordinate.

- Not being afraid to take two or three sessions to finish the job in complicated cases.

Conducting a productive interview for goal setting calls for as much detailed planning as the job and the benefits would justify.

SOME SUCCESS INDICATORS

Like goals, successes can be measured according to various criteria, largely depending upon the nature of the work the organization is involved in.

Some common means of measuring success include:

Quantity

1. Number of patients treated
2. Number of items processed (orders, forms)
3. Number of cases handled (referrals, complaints)
4. Number of lab tests processed
5. Percentage of employees participating (in various programs)
6. Percentage of employees absent (or late, or complaining)

Quality

1. Error rate
2. Hours lost to injuries (severity rate)
3. Percentage of orders without an error
4. Turnover rate of employees
5. Percentage of tests repeated
6. Percentage of work redone (or rejected)
7. Percentage of downtime or unproductive time

Time

1. Number or percentage of deadlines missed
2. Number of days to complete
3. Turnaround time
4. Number of working days
5. Frequency per day, week, month

Cost

1. Percent variance from budget
2. Dollars saved over previous period
3. Dollars cost per work unit
4. Number of hours to complete a task

PRESENT OR FUTURE THRUST?

A basic question to all managers is: "How can I maintain an acceptable record of performance on current operations and still be able to anticipate future problems?"

There are some differences in emphasis that must be understood.

Operations involves	*Planning involves*
Unit goals related to organizational goals	Strategy and new goals
Previous experience as a base	New variables
Functional and professional perspective (means)	Overall significance (ends)
Relatively short-term evidence of results	Long-term consequences
Tangible incentives to improve	Incentives diminishing with gradual change
Repetition, familiarity, confidence, security	Fewer guidelines, risks, trade-offs, wider margin for error
Benefits quite obvious	Benefits uncertain, usually postponable

A PLANNING PRIMER

Planning is an important—even essential—process. It need not be an inordinately trying one.

Planning, in the most basic of terms, involves six steps:

1. Defining goals
   a. Be brief
   b. Put them in writing
   c. Be specific
   d. Be sure they're measurable

2. Collecting all relevant data
   a. Consider the best methods
   b. Take changed circumstances or conditions into account

3. Selecting the best method
   a. Eliminate unnecessary steps
   b. Simplify
   c. Determine priorities

4. Developing the plan
   a. Select and train people
   b. Provide the necessary resources
   c. Eliminate the obstacles

5. Implementing the plan
   a. Revise as necessary

6. Following up
   a. Be persistent

WHY PLANNING IS RESISTED

Many individuals and organizations resist the all-important task of planning. Why?

Because *personally* we are:

- Bored by the predictable
- Anxious to be in control
- Limited in self-confidence

- Inclined to overlook shortcomings
- Undecided about our personal goals
- Hestitant to change

Because *organizationally* we are:

- Preoccupied with present problems
- Intrigued by the unknown, but afraid of the uncertain
- Fearful about failure
- Pressed for time
- Lacking information
- Apprehensive about decisions that may be wrong

GAUGING THE ENVIRONMENT

Every experienced manager knows that there are intangible, yet nonetheless real, elements that affect his or her operations. These "intangibles" are encountered somewhere between the development of objectives and their fulfillment.

Successful managers generally are able to sense what will—and what will not—work in their organizations, within what different groups, and at what different levels. They know what they can sell to their people and what they cannot.

Such managers also learn to understand and adjust to certain facts of their organization's particular "life style." They learn, for example, to cope with the fact that some units will be slower in implementing new programs than others; that certain communications will break down or misfire; that some units can never seem to get going without prodding.

And every organization develops its own unique environment, or climate. Upon closer scrutiny, we can determine that the nature of this climate is the result of the interaction between two major sets of conditions:

1. There is the relatively controllable aspect—such things as the organizational structure and other formalized management practices, policies, and procedures.

2. There is a more unpredictable set of conditions which consists of people and the ways in which they react to, utilize, and otherwise get around these formalized organizational elements.

How managers and other employees perceive these formal and informal "ingredients" affects their actions on the job. This naturally influences overall organizational performance.

QUESTIONS FOR PLANNERS

Planners need to be constantly aware of their unique and vital contribution to the organizations they serve.

Answers to questions such as the following will give a manager some direction for his or her planning:

- What can I personally do to make the greatest impact on the organization?
- What new and smarter ways can I find to do the job?
- What are my subordinates' ideas?
- Have I explored the full range of possibilities before discarding any idea?
- What roadblocks need to be eliminated?
- Have I determined how much time is involved in completing my proposal(s)?

In terms of team performance, each manager also should ask:

- What direction do I need to give my team to ensure that its activities contribute directly to area performance?
- What am I or my team doing that has nothing to do with my objectives or that even may be working against them?
- What am I doing that is being duplicated elsewhere?

FROM PAPER PLANS TO ACTION

The best of plans is only as good as it works when put into action. It may be helpful to trace the process of moving from one stage to the other.

Persistent Middle-Management Problems. The most persistent of middle-management problem areas are (1) the efficient application of technical skill, (2) the systematic ordering of operations, and (3) the organization of sustained cooperation (teamwork). If these are out of balance, no other virtues will compensate, and the operation as a whole will not be successful.

Interpret Your Plan as You Go. There is a need to interpret plans in accordance with their purpose. Sometimes this requires modification, but with care. Plans are subject to change in detail, and part of nearly every plan has to be reedited in light of more recent events as action proceeds.

Divide and Conquer. Two hints may be helpful in overcoming procrastination:

1. Commit yourself. Having promised performance by a certain date, you will find yourself honor-bound to meet it.
2. Do not tackle an accumulation of work like a bulldozer. Break the pile down into small, accessible units, and grapple with them one by one.

Schedule Sub-Jobs. When a plan reaches the action stage, it is necessary to assign proportions and priorities as far as possible. The major schedule will be set in the master planning: completion by a certain date. There remains the detailed scheduling so that all parts fit into the ultimate whole.

Functions. Distribute the functions involved in the jobs according to time. Working back from the targeted completion date, determine what must be done today, tomorrow, etc. Sequence is vital. If the nature of the job does not dictate the order in which operations must be done, perform the most essential ones first.

Simplify Layout. The best role for the supervisor is to put useful tools where they can be found quickly and easily. Streamline your work. Allow as few hindrances as possible.

Integrate Effort. In order to integrate effort, keep all affected parties fully briefed. Share your work. Delegate what you can to others, and cooperate with those in other departments.

Act with Precision. It is good practice to deliberate with caution but act with decision and promptness.

Seek Better Ways. Anticipation is just as important as the capability to handle crises. When you have had a job in process for a reasonable period of time, take a look at it to see if there is an easier or more efficient way of doing it. Group activities so that one follows another with the least interruption and effort. An even pace, rather than a series of spurts, makes the best use of your energy.

Get on with It! There is only one direction in which you can coast—downhill. It takes more effort to *get* going than to *keep* going. In his book *The Technique of Getting Things Done*, Dr. Donald A. Laird wrote: "Don't look at a thing: start it. Don't put it off a day: start it. Don't pretend you must think it over: start it. Don't start half-heartedly: put everything you can muster into your start."

TESTING IDEAS

As you proceed with your planning, these questions will guide you in testing your ideas:

- If fully implemented, what would be the ultimate contribution of this idea to unit performance?
- What are the chances it will be implemented if I really get behind it and push?
- Does it have application elsewhere?
- Does it conflict with another group's objectives?
- Will it help me reach my objectives?
- Are there impediments to implementing the idea?
- If there are impediments, can I eliminate them myself or do I need help?
- Who can authorize action on my idea—me, my supervisor, or someone else?
- How can I sell my idea "up the line"?
- Do I have the resources to implement my idea without impairing other individual or group objectives?
- If I need more resources, how can I get them?

As a result of this testing process, some ideas will be discarded, some will be readily accepted, and others will require further investigation and refinement. Once an idea is judged feasible, it should be put into an action plan.

Playing It Safe

Effective leaders can't lose sleep over the possible adverse results of every action they take. If they do, they'd be better off taking orders from someone else—and so would their organizations.

WHY QUALITY CIRCLES WORK

Many organizations have adopted the Quality Circle concept. Quality Circles usually work because:

- Participation is voluntary.
- Management is supportive.
- Members learn to work as a team.
- Members solve and avoid problems; they don't just identify them.
- Management is firmly committed to "people building."

LIMITATIONS OF GROUP DECISION-MAKING

There are some limitations to the quality of group decisions that should be noted. These usually reveal themselves when the group has come to believe that *concurrence and harmony* are more important than *good ideas and high standards*.

Here are some ways to recognize when a group is falling into "groupthink:"

1. Everybody in the group gets along famously. There is no disagreement. Nobody wants to be the outsider who speaks the truth or disrupts the harmonious meetings.
2. Warning signals are screened out, along with the truth.
3. The group uses rationalizations instead of taking corrective action.
4. The group stresses loyalty, teamwork, and cohesiveness over innovative ideas and quality decisions.

5. Anyone who disagrees with the majority opinion is "a bad guy."
6. People get polarized as being either for or against the group. Those who oppose the group's ideas are labeled villains or fools, and their ideas are scorned or rejected.
7. The group sets standards and enforces them upon itself.

If your management team has fallen into the error of putting harmony and agreement above quality in decision making, it may be wise to introduce some dissenters or outside views.

ANY INNOVATIONS AVAILABLE?

The family had recently moved to town. They overslept one morning, and the seven-year-old son missed his school bus. The mother, though late for a meeting, agreed to drive him if he would direct her.

They rode several blocks before he told her to turn the first time, several more before he indicated another turn. This went on for twenty-five minutes—but when they finally reached the school, it proved to be only a short distance from their home.

Asked why he had led his mother over such a roundabout route, the child explained: "That's the way the school bus goes, and it's the only way I know."

How often have you overlooked a "better way" in favor of "the way it has always been done"?

EIGHT STEPS TO NEW IDEAS

Everyone has the ability to originate ideas and solve problems. The process is rather simple. It is based on the way our minds combine separate ideas to create new ones.

Problem solutions and new ideas are created by changing old ideas or experiences, by processing or manipulating them. We combine them in new ways, put them in a new context of time or place, add other ideas, take something away, change their meaning or purpose. We may do this accidentally and unconsciously, or we may do it deliberately and intentionally.

The question is: How do we go about this in a systematic and fruitful manner? What is the process of working with experience to produce new ideas or to solve new problems?

1. *Name the target.* What's the problem? What kind of idea do you need?
2. *Get the facts.* Pile up all the information you can about the problem, including unsuccessful attempts to solve it. Often, ideas that have failed one time will succeed at another time with a slight modification.
3. *Try the obvious solutions first.* Sometimes, merely naming a problem and collecting data about it will suggest solutions.
4. *Try the wild ideas.* In particular, look for apparently trivial, irrelevant aspects of the problem.
5. *Think intensely about the problem.* This is not really a separate step, but part of the steps we've mentioned before. Make yourself think about the problem until you have a solution or until you have reached a state of frustration.
6. *Walk away from the problem.* Put the matter out of your mind. If you have covered Steps 1-5, your subconscious usually will take over.
7. *Seize the flash of insight.* Generally, at some indefinite time after you have walked away from the problem, an answer will well up in your mind. Seize the idea at that moment and put it on paper.
8. *Do something about the idea.* Above all, don't give up. We tend to get discouraged too easily. In the pursuit of an idea, the odds are all in favor of running into periods of discouragement, times when nothing goes right, times when it appears that an answer will never come. Don't give in until you have the problem licked.

Soliciting Employee Ideas

Sometimes, being closer to the situation on a daily basis, an employee is able to come up with a better solution or idea than his or her superior. Take advantage of that.

If you have some problems or need some new ideas, ask for the employees' help. But when soliciting employee ideas:

- Managers should clearly define the issues on which they are seeking employee input.
- Managers should thoroughly explain the relevant details and why the employees' input is requested.

- An atmosphere of mutual trust must be established.
- Feedback to employees at various stages of the process is essential.
- Management must be prepared to act on employee input after it is given and in such a way that the employees will see that their input has been honestly considered.

DEVELOPING INNOVATIVE OBJECTIVES

It seems natural to think of innovations when considering goals. To help clarify innovative goals, let's review the other two job-related goals: the routine goal and the problem-oriented goal.

A *routine* goal is repetitive and concerns result areas which are ongoing, where the output is achieved over and over again. The commitment contained in the routine goal statement is simply a description of the standards or levels of performance that are considered par for the course.

Problem-oriented objectives deal with those result areas in which present performance levels fall below the accepted norm. The commitment sought in this goal statement is to a solution.

An *innovative* goal deals with a third type of result. Innovative goals deal with changes, with new things, with different outputs, either because they are being sought for the first time or because they are unique, special, one-shot affairs. You will know you're in the innovative area whenever your initial thoughts involve the use of words like develop, initiate, inaugurate, implement, begin, design, create, study, rewrite, reorganize, rearrange, or re- almost anything.

Innovative goals are the opposite of routine goals because they are not expected to be repetitive. They sometimes are suggested by problem situations since they sometimes make a contribution to remedying unsatisfactory performance, but they are distinct in that they should describe new results.

When negotiating these goals, it is desirable that the commitment be not only to develop, begin, study, etc., but to *accomplish* something as a *result* of what you develop, begin, study, etc. We don't seek change for the sake of change, but to bring about some payoff or benefits.

Perhaps the chart in Table 4-7 will help you to understand the various types of objectives even better.

Table 4-7. FOUR TYPES OF OBJECTIVES

	ROUTINE	PROBLEM-SOLVING	INNOVATIVE	PERSONAL DEVELOPMENT
HOME EXAMPLE	Cut grass and sharpen lawn mower	Fight crabgrass and dandelions	Install astroturf	Take course in organic farming
CITY EXAMPLE	Provide police and fire protection	Reduce traffic congestion in downtown area	Develop a community service council	Take a field trip to another city
HOSPITAL EXAMPLE	Process 250 lab specimens per shift	Fill 100% of budgeted nursing positions	Install a new billing procedure	Attend MBO Workshop

FORMAT FOR AN INNOVATIVE GOAL

There are four items that are likely to be included in any statement of an innovative goal: Idea, Results, Method, and Timetable. Perhaps the Innovative Goal Worksheet in Table 4-8 will help you commit your idea to paper more effectively. Each of the four items reflected on this worksheet requires full consideration and negotiation.

Idea

Write down innovative idea at the head of the worksheet. Notice that this is not the goal—only the idea. It is the name of the project you have in mind.

Results

The actual goal or output is the desired improvement that set you to thinking. What is the payoff you expect? What are the con-

Table 4-8. INNOVATIVE GOAL WORKSHEET

1. Innovative Idea: _____

   _____

2. Desired Results: _____

   _____

3. Method:	4. Timetable:
_____	_____
_____	_____
_____	_____
_____	_____
_____	_____
_____	_____
_____	_____

crete improvements/benefits that will warrant the expenditure of time, money, and energy to implement this idea? Outputs are the only justification for spending the organization's resources.

Method and Timetable

To achieve any benefits, there always are certain associated costs. Every innovative goal statement is a small cost-benefits comparison. The question you must ask—and answer—is: "How much are you willing to spend to attain the specified benefit(s)?" If the cost is too high, you might be better off to forego the results.

Costs are itemized under the columns "Method" and "Timetable." They include not just dollars, but all resources associated with the innovation—time costs, energy costs, people costs, opportunity costs, frustration costs. After the initial costs, there are maintenance costs, policing costs, and (possibly) abandonment costs.

Method should cover all of the steps which will be necessary to implement and track the innovation: actions and expenditures, listed step by step. Beside each item in this schedule of events, under the "Timetable" column, a time period or completion date should be listed. A final completion date is not enough if you are to monitor progress throughout the implementation period.

Some examples of innovative results are listed in Table 4-9.

It is important to know when to abandon a project. Often, what seems like a good idea turns out to be unworkable. We have to know when things outlive their usefulness or when they don't live up to their promise. Even if the results are achieved, it is possible that the idea will fail because the costs (of one type or another) are too high. Costs should be weighed on a fairly regular basis to see that they do not begin to outweigh the benefits.

Remember to differentiate between the idea and the goal. The goal is what we are after, not the idea.

WHY ORGANIZATIONS
LOSE THEIR EFFECTIVENESS

It is natural that each department in an organization should attempt to create order so as to gain efficiency. These routines

Table 4-9. EXAMPLES OF INNOVATIVE RESULTS

IDEA	RESULTS
Reorganized the department	equitable workload enlarge span of control
Conduct a feasibility study	potential income potential monitoring
Install a new service	at what cost criteria of success
Automate an operation	save money, people add information
Research a community service	need to be met cost/benefit
Design a new procedure	time or cost saving with what specs?
Replace a machine	quantity, quality cost
Conduct a survey	of whom? on what?
Forecast something	accuracy timeliness
Prepare a report	completeness acceptability w/o rewrite
Present new education program	documented shortage/need public impact

become firmly set, and little slows down their development. In time, each department builds higher and higher barriers to prevent outsiders from disturbing those routines.

What can be done?

Rigid and excessive routines can be prevented by introducing continuous change. Top management must:

1. Recognize the dangers of rigidity.
2. Create, as much as possible, departments that can handle the entire workflow toward an end product.
3. Continually watch those areas where interdepartmental cooperation is necessary, making certain that it is working and that one department isn't overpowering the other.

4. Give managers credit in performance reviews for working effectively with other departments.

5. Use a mediator to work out serious departmental squabbles.

6. Transfer people occasionally from one department to another so they can get an overview and learn to understand the workings of the other departments.

7. Periodically create change so that rigidity is discouraged and people are encouraged to adapt and grow.

WHY SOME MANAGERS PERFORM POORLY

When managers do not perform as well as they should, it may be due to a physical or emotional problem. These possibilities should never be overlooked.

On the other hand, there may be some other, and more easily corrected, cause:

- Does not know what is expected.
- Does not know how he or she is doing.
- Cannot do the work.
- Will not do the work.
- Lacks organizational support.
- Has a poor relationship with the boss.

Each of these situations, once discovered, can be corrected. The one thing that is *never* acceptable is an excuse.

5

Managing Situations

Difficult situations which occur from time to time generally stem from one cause: Some part of "the machinery" isn't functioning as it is supposed to.

It is a manager's role to monitor this "machinery" continuously to see that such breakdowns do not occur. Among the key management areas which must be monitored are:

- Poor planning
- Unmeasurable goals
- Inadequate controls
- Increasing costs
- Ineffective management development
- Poor communication
- Ineffective delegation
- Low morale

- Too much change
- Too little change

Many of these subjects are discussed in earlier sections of this book. Some of them may bear reviewing at regular intervals— or, at least, as new problems arise.

REDUCING RESISTANCE TO CHANGE

Most of us don't change for the sake of change but because we see a definite need for improvement or see how things should be in the future.

The ability to motivate others to accept change, when it is necessary, is extremely valuable. This involves:

1. Realizing that others may not share your beliefs or approve of your attitudes.
2. Realizing that the beliefs and attitudes of others are the result of habit patterns.
3. Visualizing the change from the standpoint of those who will have to use or adapt to it.
4. Anticipating difficulties in gaining acceptance, and devising ways to make the transition more acceptable.
5. Carefully considering all of the consequences of the change. Abrupt, sweeping changes can be quite disruptive—sometimes disastrous. It always is best to bring about changes gradually, a step at a time.
6. Recognizing that any significant change triggers emotional tension— either because old behavior is found to be inadequate or because new behavior may be required. Dissipating this tension may take some time. A clear incentive to change, where it is possible to offer one, helps those who are affected to do so.
7. Talking with key people involved before you implement a change. If you can enlist their support, you may encounter much less resistance later on.
8. Maintaining continuing contact (communication) with employees as the change is made. Affected individuals should know what will be different, and why. Avoid surprises.

SELLING AN UNPOPULAR IDEA

Nearly every manager has faced a situation in which it became necessary to "bite the bullet" and do something that would be unpopular. In such situations, it's often necessary to gain the acceptance, if not the support, of others—to "sell" the unpopular idea to an audience that's basically hostile to it.

Here are a few ways in which you can "sugarcoat the pill":

1. Use as much forewarning time as possible.
2. Be willing to bend and modify on small points.
3. Find out what the other person really wants in the situation, then find a way to meet that need without giving up or backing down on the basic idea.
4. Trade off something the other person wants as a part of the arrangement.
5. If you must reduce the responsibilities or actual functions of people, use physical things like desks, telephones, and the like to raise their status.
6. Find out who is the most likely to be rebellious and put him or her in charge of implementing the change.
7. Listen carefully to what the other person says, and demonstrate that you understand both what the person is saying and what he or she is feeling. Then look for trading stock.
8. Avoid the things that surely will alienate and ruffle everyone, such as giving them a flat-out order. It may seem gutsy and dynamic to order people to "do it because I want it done," but it builds up resistance.
9. Don't blame decisions on someone above you.
10. Before a general announcement is made, be sure to explain all major changes that will affect people to those individuals, face to face, one by one. Don't let people read about unfavorable changes in the local newspaper, the house organ, or a policy memo dropped in their mail slot.

TEN RULES OF PERSUASION

Persuasion is a talent. It requires tact, finesse, sensitivity, and timing. Here are some tips on how to increase your persuasiveness:

1. Give your conclusion up front.

2. Don't be afraid to appeal to emotions.

3. Expect resistance and try to anticipate what it will be so that you can respond to it at the appropriate time.

4. Don't be afraid to repeat yourself.

5. Talk about the features of your plan, demonstrating all of the details and the fine points.

6. Describe the benefits of the plan in the terms of the listener, whether that is the boss, the division, or the entire company.

7. Use all of the time available for your presentation.

8. Show how the desired action is possible, and try to answer *in advance* any suggestion that it is not.

9. Be frank about telling your listener what your own motives are.

10. Be factual or you will lose credibility.

Intercept Those Interruptions

Everyone has had the experience of being deep in thought, late for an appointment, or sitting in an important meeting and . . . there's an interruption. The train of thought is lost. You never get to the appointment. You lose the continuity and momentum of the meeting, and usually for something of little or no consequence.

With proper safeguards, that sort of thing should never happen. Here's what you can do:

Visitors: scheduled and unscheduled

Problem	Solution
1. Your ego. It makes you feel important to be asked for advice or to have social drop-ins.	Recognize the problem. Make yourself available at lunch.
2. A desire to keep informed, to stay on the grapevine.	Get your information in a planned, more certain basis.
3. Fear of offending.	Don't be oversensitive. Keep a time log to show you just how intrusive those interruptions can be.

Problem	Solution
4. Ineffective screening.	Train your secretary to screen visitors and calls without offending.
5. Ineffective monitoring of overlong visits and calls.	Set a time limit for each visit, and call (but be flexible when something important arises). A wrist-alarm is a self-reminder. If you prefer, your secretary can interrupt to get you back on schedule.
6. Making decisions below your level.	Make only the decisions your subordinates can't.
7. Requiring or expecting your subordinates to "check with you" excessively.	Manage by exception.
8. Failure to delegate.	Do nothing that can be delegated. (Review the material on delegation in Chapter 3.)
9. Desire to socialize.	Do it elsewhere.
10. No provision for "availability."	Include a "quiet hour" in each day's schedule. Implement a modified "open-door" policy.
11. Encouraging staff to bring you their problems.	This not only encourages dropping in, but dependence. Encourage initiative, risk taking, decision making.

Telephone Calls

Problem	Solution
1. No secretary.	Have the switchboard screen your calls. Use a cutoff switch.
2. To appear available.	Call back within a reasonable time.
3. Enjoy socializing.	Do it someplace else.
4. Lack self-discipline.	Learn to group your calls, handle them in bunches.
5. To remain informed and involved.	Accomplish this in a planned and more certain manner.
6. Poor screening.	Train your secretary to intercept and divert.

Problem	Solution
7. Ego.	Recognize it and control it.
8. Misdirected calls.	Train the telephone people to do the job right.
9. Lack of coordination.	Delegate.
10. Unable to terminate a call.	Practice being brief. Say, "Thanks for calling" or "I'm sorry, I have another call."
11. Fear of offending.	Don't be oversensitive.

Meeting

Problem	Solution
1. Lack of purpose.	Instruct subordinates that no meeting should be held without a need.
2. Lack of agenda.	Insist that everyone calling a meeting prepare an agenda.
3. Wrong or too many people present.	Insist that only those who need to attend be invited.
4. Wrong time.	Insure opportune timing.
5. Wrong place.	Select a location consistent with the objectives of the meeting. It should be free from interruptions, necessary physical equipment should be on hand, and it should require minimum travel for the majority of the people.
6. Too many meetings.	Test the need for regular meetings. Don't hold them occasionally, just to see what happens. Or cut the normal meeting time in half.
7. Inadequate motive.	A call for a meeting should provide written notice containing all essentials, including the expected contribution and the materials necessary for preparation.

Problem	Solution
8. Not starting on time.	Start on time. Do not penalize those who arrive on time and reward those who are late.
9. Socializing.	Get down to business. Socialize elsewhere.
10. Allowing interruptions.	Set a policy and let everyone know that interruptions are not to be tolerated. Have someone take messages and deliver them during a coffee break or at lunch.
11. Wandering from the agenda.	Let it be known that you expect and demand that the agenda be followed. Announcing a termination time may help.
12. Failure to end on time.	Timing and agenda—for each item as well as the final time for adjournment—will help to keep the meeting on schedule.
13. Indecision.	Keep your objective in mind and move toward it.
14. Deciding without adequate information.	Be sure the necessary information will be available before you schedule the meeting.
15. Failure to summarize conclusions and record minutes.	Summarize conclusions to insure agreement and remind participants of assignments. Record decisions, assignments, and deadlines in the minutes, which should be distributed within one day of the meeting.
16. Failure to follow up.	List uncompleted items under "Unfinished Business" at the beginning of the next agenda. Request status reports until the work is completed.
17. Failure to terminate committees when their business has ended.	Keep an inventory of all committees. Abolish those whose missions have been accomplished.

Table 5-1. THE NATURAL "BREAKS"

PROJECT OR ASSIGNMENT TO BE COMPLETED	CHOSEN CALENDAR- BREAK DATES	NEW PROJECT OR ASSIGNMENT TO BE STARTED

As you look at each day's schedule, you will see that there are natural breaks there too. If there is a short time between two scheduled blocks of time, what tasks would be appropriate to use the time to greatest benefit? _____

_____

_____

Which things can be handled while you are waiting for an appointment?

_____

Which tasks could be handled during travel time? _____

_____

Consider these transitional times carefully. Some tasks can be adapted to make use of time that would otherwise be *lost*.

As you look at each day's schedule, you will see that there are natural breaks there, too. If there is a short period between two scheduled blocks of time, how can you use it to greatest benefit? What can you accomplish while waiting for an appointment? Which tasks can be handled during travel time?

AVOID COMMUNICATION CONFUSION

There is an increasing need for information. We must learn if we are to survive. We are bombarded with messages from morning until night, and the subject matter is increasingly complex. Communication is not precise. Neither is language. There is a variety of languages, as well as vocabularies, pertaining to various subjects and professions. There are sign languages, the language of gestures and inflections, and "body language." We cram our communications with unneeded information. Talk is cheap, so we spend it recklessly.

Is there any wonder there's often confusion, even when we are trying our best to communicate?

Try to be alert to each of the following:

1. *Self-defense systems.* We build barriers to defend ourselves. We *assume* what others are intending to say, so we stop listening. We hurtle to get to the ending ahead of the communicator. We interpret, interpolate, fill in, and prejudice.

2. *Sender's view of the situation.* One's view is no substitute for accurate observation, validity, and reliability.

3. *Sender's view of the receiver.* Our opinions of people can color the form, nature, and content of our communications.

4. *Meanings* can vary, depending on the manner in which they are expressed and the context in which they are used.

5. *Choice of medium.* Some media automatically convey a sense of greater urgency and importance than others. A *written* message is surer and more lasting than an oral one. Confucius points out: "I hear and I forget, I see and I remember, I do and I understand."

6. *Related and associated messages.* Inflections, gestures, expressions, body movement, and actions all tend to add to—or take away from—the message you are attempting to convey.

7. *Interference.* To be successful, your message must *get through.*

8. *Receiver's views.* The recipient will not receive the message accurately if he allows it to become distorted by his opinion of the sender, the subject, the medium, or some personal bias.

9. *Receipt and translation.* An effective message must be received, decoded, translated, and examined.

10. *Feedback.* The circuit is not complete until a message has been received, understood, and acknowledged.

SENDING AND RECEIVING GOOD FEEDBACK

Feedback is only one form of communication, but like all others, it is important . . . and it can be misused. The April 1982 issue of *Training* magazine offered some suggestions.

Getting feedback

1. Ask for feedback only from people who can give you a balanced report. Make sure you trust and respect them enough to accept their feedback.
2. Tell the source of your feedback exactly what behavior or performance you want feedback on, why you want it, and what you will do with it.
3. Ask for feedback in a neutral fashion.
4. Tell the individual how you will respond to the feedback.
5. When you receive feedback, you can ask clarifying questions, but do not put your source on the spot. Saying, "Could you say that in another way?" or "Could you give me an example?" is better than saying, "What do you mean by *that*?"
6. Focus on open-ended, future-oriented questions, such as "What could I do to keep that from happening next time?"
7. Tell the resource person what the payoff is for him or her. If there is risk, it must be worth taking.

Giving Feedback

1. Good feedback is solicited, not imposed, and it deals with a specific performance the inquirer wants information on.
2. Good feedback separates perceptions and facts.
3. Good feedback includes a balance of positive and negative.
4. Good feedback is specific and clear. Try to avoid qualifiers and disclaimers, and certainly avoid gossip, rumors, scuttlebutt, and opinions— unless they are asked for.
5. Good feedback deals with things that can be changed.
6. Avoid emotional, biased words.
7. Provide the feedback at an appropriate time, but don't give it hastily.
8. Check the message *received* to make sure it coincides with the message *sent*.

9. Let the receiver decide how to change. In other words, don't tell the other person what to do, unless asked.

10. Leave out anything you're unsure of—unless you identify it as such.

REASONS TO PUT IT IN WRITING

Verbal communication and individuals' memories often (perhaps usually) are inadequate. But there are a number of other reasons why a message should be committed to writing:

- To remind or refresh the memory.
- To allow time to reread, absorb, consider, and appraise facts or ideas.
- To document occurrences and guidelines for future planning.
- To assure accuracy of records.
- To give or receive orders or instructions.
- To prepare reports.
- To clarify thinking.
- To prevent misunderstandings.
- To save time.
- To plan ahead.
- To organize.
- To state an agreement or to confirm one.
- To keep lists of facts, addresses, dates, figures, etc.
- To keep track of what has been read or said.

WHAT SUCCESSFUL WRITERS DO

Many people think of writing as a burdensome task, which may account for why they do it too seldom, too hastily, too badly disorganized, or too ineffectively.

1. Start with a rough outline.
2. Reserve enough time to complete your first draft. You may try dictating it, if that's more comfortable.

3. Refrain from rewriting until you have finished the first draft.

4. Don't try to be impressive by using big words, long sentences, flowery phrases, or an evasive style.

5. Edit and rewrite.

6. Do it over and over, if necessary, until you are satisfied with the result.

RUMOR RELIEVERS

Rumors are another form of communication—and one of the worst. You can alleviate rumors by:

- Realizing that people are going to think and talk about things that affect them and their jobs.
- Avoiding a secretive attitude. Hush-hush items are always interesting and subject to speculation.
- Deciding if it is really *important* to keep a secret.
- Deciding if it's really *possible* to keep a secret.
- Giving people legitimate work-related news to talk about.
- Putting the facts on the table promptly, and making them available to everyone.
- Not "keeping something quiet" without good, valid reasons. And when you're making that decision, think several times about those reasons.

> It
> topples
> governments,
> wrecks
> marriages,
> ruins
> careers,
> busts
> reputations,
> causes
> heartaches,
> nightmares,
> indigestion,
> spawns suspicion,
> generates
> grief,
> dispatches

innocent
people
to cry in their
pillows.
Even its name
hisses.
It's called
gossip.
Office gossip,
Shop gossip.
Party gossip.
It makes
headlines
and headaches.
Before
you repeat
a story,
ask yourself:
Is it true?
Is it fair?
Is it necessary?
If not,
shut up.
United Technologies Corp.

GIVING ASSIGNMENTS

There are two contrasting styles of giving out assignments.
Managers who tell not merely what they want done, but exactly
how they want it done are:

- Guilty of overkill, not management.
- Robbing their people of a chance to use their own brains, judgment,
  and initiative.

Those who manage by objectives *negotiate* the desired results, but
don't tell people how to do their jobs. This:

- Keeps subordinates interested.
- Lets them have the satisfaction of working out solutions.
- Encourages creativity and innovation.

When employees are encouraged to think for themselves, they are happier, they work better, and they reward the organization with more good ideas.

THE GAME OF "PASS THE BUCK"

Red Rover, Red Rover, let the excuses come over! That's the principle of buck passing. Making excuses. Dodging blame. Avoiding responsibility. But there are as many variations of the game as there are to solitaire. In October 1982, *Supervisory Management* magazine described several of them. How many of these have you heard?

"He did it." Placing the blame on someone else.

Hot potato. Shifting the spotlight to something else.

Cry wolf. Listing the negative consequences of your involvement.

Somewhere over the rainbow. Shifting attention from today's problems by suggesting that success is "just around the corner."

Hide 'n seek. Clouding the issue so that no one is held responsible.

Quick-change artist. Changing the rules when the effort does not meet expectations.

Chicken. Letting somebody else risk the failure.

Blind man's bluff. Using unfamiliar language, jargon, or complex statistics to communicate the status of a project.

Witch hunt. Finding problems, even when they don't matter.

Acts of god. Used to explain inaction or failure to meet a goal. Often used to excuse several months of inactivity.

SOLVING PROBLEMS

Problem-solving goals involve areas which are not measuring up to the accepted norm. Effective managers are constantly looking for such problem areas so that they can be handled *before* they get out of hand and *before* a crisis arises.

The following process will enable you to separate, identify, and work through a problem:

1. Make a brief statement of the problem—no longer than two sentences. For example: "I am dissatisfied with the current level of ___." Take only five minutes to do this.

2. Find out the facts of the matter. *What* is the present level of performance?

3. What would be an acceptable level of performance?

4. How did you arrive at the "acceptable" level (industry norms, professional standards, previous achievement)? Be realistic in establishing the desired level of performance.

5. What are some of the possible causes contributing to the present unsatisfactory levels of operation? Brainstorm this point. Come up with as long a list as you can.

6. Of these, which are the *most likely* causes?

7. What are some alternative solutions or courses of action? Brainstorm again. List your ideas without evaluating them.

8. What criterion (criteria) will you use to evaluate these possible solutions?
   a. How much will it contribute to arriving at the desired level of performance?
   b. Is the net financial impact after costs balanced against anticipated benefits?
   c. What is the feasibility of the idea in light of physical capability, company policy, other consequences?
   d. What time is involved?
   e. What will be the impact on morale?

9. How would an *ideal* solution score against these criteria?

10. "Score" each potential solution.

11. Determine what course of action is called for to solve the problem. This might include a *combination* of ideas to result in the *best* solution— that which is closest to the *ideal*.

12. Write out a Time and Action Plan using your chosen solution(s); add target dates for beginning, completing, and evaluating the action. This becomes your commitment; but if the passing of time reveals that a problem still exists, *go back to the drawing board.*

Problem example

1. *Statement of Problem:* I am dissatisfied with the current level of retail receivables in our division.

2. *Present Level:* 47 days of sales outstanding.

3. *Reasonable Desired Level:* 42-40 days of sales outstanding.

4. *Basis for Estimate of Desired Level:* Previous historical data. Impact on profit position.

5. *Possible Causes:*
   a. Attitude of retail manager—considers it low priority.
   b. Lacks knowledge of tools to handle this area.
   c. Systems flow problems.
   d. Inadequate staff.
   e. Administers policies inconsistently.
   f. Location and size of operation.

6. *Most Likely Causes*
   Attitude of retail manager—considers it low priority.
   Systems flow problems.

7. *Alternative solution*
   (Options)

8. *Criteria for evaluating*	*Contribution*	*Cost*	*Feasibility*
9. *The Ideal Score*	H	L	H
10. *Score for Each Option*	H	H	L
a. Increase staff	H	H	L
b. Take management course	M	L	H
c. Training of manager in the importance of profit (and cash flow)	M	L	H
d. Dollar incentives	M	H	L
e. Communications	H	L	H
f. Organize his or her operation	L	L	H
g. Team to study systems	M	H	H
h. Data processing output	H	H	H
i. Clerical load reduced	M	L	H
j. Reduce approvals	H	H	H
k. Service bureau (versus in-house)	H	H	H
l. Improved controls	H	L	H

11. *Best Solution(s) Most Nearly Meeting the Ideal:* l, e, b, c, i.

12. *Time and Action Plan*
    l. Adopt control system used in Garden Division within 90 days.
    e. Include article on receivables in each monthly edition of dealer magazine for next 12 months.
    b. Send 10 worst offenders to appropriate management course within 3 months.

c. Bring in new Receivable Manager from Garden Division within 30 days.

i. Add another clerical position in the department immediately. Review when new system becomes operative.

MAKING A DECISION

As you have just seen, problem solving involves decision making, and there are eight basic steps to making a decision:

1. *Define the problem.* State primary and secondary aims. Examine the things to be accomplished thoroughly, making them broad and general.

2. *Redefine the problem.* Be more specific. Translate your general aims into quantitative goals. Specify time, dollars, units. Intersperse the subgoals among the main goals.

3. *See how your goals fit in the overall organizational goals.* Make your goals conform to those of the organization. Don't give high priority to something the company considers low priority.

4. *Line up alternatives.* Judge them against your instinctive choice, if you have one. Consider every alternative objectively. Look for the foreseeable consequences of each alternative.

5. *Review resources.* Each alternative takes time, money, and manpower. How much of each do you have to apply? How much will you have six months from now? Inventory the resources needed for each alternative and compare them to those you have available.

6. *List and evaluate the consequences should the decision turn out incorrectly.* Do this for each possible alternative—and for the decision to do nothing at all.

7. *Sell the decision.* Talk with key people about your alternatives. Get relevant information and opinions. Try to draw out objections and obstacles.

8. *Decide and implement.* By word and action, make everyone aware of your continuing commitment to the plan you have developed.

WHY PROBLEMS AREN'T SOLVED

Some problems seem to defy solution. Some linger within a company through several generations of management. Why?

- Subordinates often will not criticize their supervisors.
- People tend to be self-protective of their positions and their hopes for promotion.
- The presence of people with technical expertise tends to intimidate those who are afraid of admitting their ignorance.
- A sense of urgency often stimulates unreliable judgments.
- Personal conflicts often work against constructive, cooperative problem solving.
- People tend to see problems from their own points of view, rather than from the broader organizational perspective.
- Focusing on a distasteful situation clouds the atmosphere with tension, fear, and uncertainty—often for both parties.

STEP-BY-STEP DECISION MAKING

Decision making is important to every manager. It is a form of problem solving, and it makes use of innovative ideas.

Four steps are involved:

1. Analyzing the problem.
2. Finding alternative solutions.
3. Analyzing and comparing those alternatives.
4. Choosing the best alternative.

In Figure 5-1 there is a graphic representation of the decision-making process.

WHY PEOPLE ARE LATE

Few things are more frustrating to the busy executive than wasting time because people are late. When people are late to a meeting, for example, they hurt themselves (by missing potentially valuable information) and they hurt the others.

At best, tardiness is rude.

DECISION-MAKING PROCESS CHART

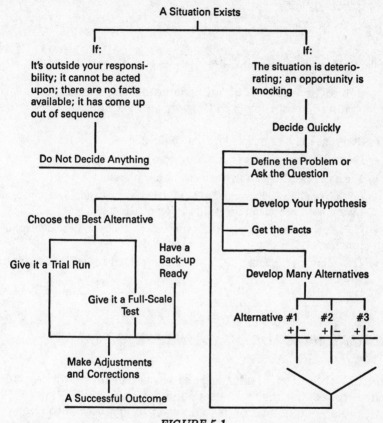

FIGURE 5-1

Why, then, are some people almost habitually late? The July 1983 issue of *The Inside Executive* offered these explanations:

1. *Rebellion.* They're secretly trying to beat a system that prizes efficiency.

2. *Exaggerated self-importance.* By being late, they are "proving" that they are busy and important.

3. *Fear or uncertainty.* They are attempting to avoid what they expect to find on arrival.

215

4. *Attention.* To some people, being late is a way to get noticed.

5. *Manipulation.* Such people are using time as a weapon to convey their authority.

POWER POINTS FOR INFLUENCING OTHERS

In order to be effective at influencing others, it is important to understand some of the psychology of motivation.

- Everyone can be motivated in some fashion.
- People tend to do things for *their* reasons, not yours.
- The overextension of a strength can be a weakness.

  In the final analysis, you do NOT motivate people. You create an environment in which they will be *self*-motivated.

- If I know more about you than you know about me, I can control our communication.
- If I know more about you than you know about yourself, I can control you.

TEN PRINCIPLES FOR IMPROVING PERFORMANCE

The first obligation of managers is to sustain their unit's performance—to see that the work gets done.

The second obligation is to do everything possible to *improve* the unit's performance. These principles might be helpful to you in attempting to do that:

1. In any decision-making situation, those who will be affected by it should be informed and, when appropriate, consulted.

2. The goals of the organization should be clearly understood by those who will do the work.

3. The goals of individuals should be negotiated in a manner consistent with the goals of the organization.

4. When responsibility is delegated, corresponding authority (with reasonable limits) also should be delegated.

5. As a general rule, the responsible person who is nearest to the situation in question should make the decision.

6. Everyone in the organization must be made aware of the relationship between responsibility and competence.

7. The practice of basic courtesy is essential in building goodwill.

8. When a decision is to be reached, those who are consulted should be told the way in which their counsel will be used.

9. Favoritism, or the appearance of favoritism, is harmful to morale.

10. In dealing with problems, seek solutions, not blame.

GETTING MORE VALUE
WITHOUT ADDING COST

Inevitably, managers discover a number of things they would like to do—if they could only afford it. The "cost" can be in dollars, in manpower, in time, or in some other resource.

How can you get what you want *without paying for it*?

1. *Use somebody else's budget.* If another department has excess (or unused) dollars, manpower, etc., find a means of using it to your (and the company's) benefit.

2. *Use volunteer labor.* In training, for example, line managers often can be used as trainers.

3. *Use temporary help.* Bringing people in for seasonal jobs, special projects, or periodic overloads makes the best use of temporary and part-time people.

4. *Use committees from other departments.*

5. *Use advisory boards.*

6. *Use study groups.* Form young professionals into study groups to write position papers that explore issues, dig out facts, find missions, and present optional approaches.

7. *Use charge-backs.* A staff department is the maker and vendor of "software" to captive internal departments that should be treated as customers.

8. *Look for outside funds.* Some kinds of staff services can be sold to other, noncompeting firms. The extra revenue can help to stretch your budget.

9. *Do some lobbying.* Sell the features and benefits of your program to others who may be able to help in the financing.

10. *Create an exciting objective.* People like to "get in on" something that's exciting, innovative, and capable of producing a meaningful payoff.

11. *Improve your efficiency.* Look for methods improvement, work simplification, and new technology to increase your operational efficiency.

12. *Improve the productivity of your staff.* Rearrange responsibility by dividing labor differently. Create more flexibility in staff assignments. Find more collaboration. Ease jurisdictional disputes by lowering functional barriers between subdepartments.

13. *Use job-sharing.* Use several people to cover the same job, perhaps part-time personnel who usually work at a lower pay and benefits level than full-time employees.

GENERAL PRINCIPLES OF "MAKING DEALS"

Achieving a purpose through other individuals *not* under your authority usually means "making a deal." The September 1982 edition of *Texas Business* offered some guidelines. Follow them and you stand a better chance of coming out the winner, not the loser:

1. *Know what you want.* Don't worry about what the others get. It's self-defeating to judge by comparison. Jealously and envy are diversions and obstacles to successful people.

2. *Understand the other side of the deal.* Put yourself in the other party's place. What are their real requirements? Desires? Plans? What are they truly looking for in the deal? When a good deal is arranged, giving someone else what they want will not take away from what you want.

3. *Seek "win-win" situations.* Search for situations in which each side can achieve certain of its goals without adversely affecting the other.

4. *Avoid "hype."* Hype sometimes helps to sell one deal, but it always hinders any subsequent ones. Exaggeration is a short-term, rapidly depleting asset—and a long-term, quickly accruing liability.

5. *Address questions nobody even asked.* Nothing is more impressive than for one side to discuss sensitive subjects about itself *without being asked.* It adds tremendously to your credibility.

6. *Be fair but frank.* Don't look to gain the upper hand—but don't appear to be a doormat, either. Let the other party see that you know the game, the rules, and the players. Being fair doesn't mean being weak.

7. *Act as if the opponents to your deal will become its public relations agents.* They will. No matter how confidential a deal, other people will hear about it. Above all, never boast about "besting" someone. Your reputation is too valuable to gamble with.

REASONING WITH THOSE WHO WILL NOT REASON

Not everyone thinks as you do. If you recognize that fact, you will communicate a great deal better with your superiors, your peers, and your subordinates.

Here are a number of "stylize" thought patterns that you may encounter:

1. *Impulsive thinkers* hardly think at all. Instead, they merely react to situations. They are likely to be discipline problems.

2. *Self-protective thinkers* interpret situations in me-against-you terms. They have trouble recognizing long-term consequences.

3. *Conforming thinkers* have some conception of personal responsibility and standards, but only at a naive level. They can be useful employees when rules are well defined because they deal with life in a paint-by-the-numbers way.

While all simplistic thinkers see things in exaggerated, black-and-white terms, only impulsive thinkers are really antisocial or difficult to manipulate.

To deal with self-protective and conforming thinkers:

- Use clear-cut orders. Exaggerated, old-fashioned appeals work best, together with the strong reminder that "you know what side your bread is buttered on."

- Use easy-to-comprehend rules, even at the slight risk of sounding overly simple to other employees.

Index

L

Landry, Tom, 83-84
Lateness, 214-16
"Laws" of management, 4
Leadership ability, 13, 16-18
   rating of, 24, 139
Listening, 114-16
   failure of, 115-16
   techniques, 56-59
   understanding and, 115
Lowell, James Russell, 63

M

McClelland, David, 98
MacKenzie, R. Alex, 37
Management development, 88
Management Review, 37
Management styles:
   autocratic versus developmental, 78-83
   continuum of, 8-9
   self-appraisal of, 74
Management theory, reconciling practice and, 145
Meetings, 202-3
   time spent in, 48-49
Memory exercises, 101
Michigan, University of, 20
Mismatch versus failure, 103-4
Mission statement, 154
Morale, 94-95
More, Hannah, 172
Motivation, 93-100
   achievement and, 98
   morale and, 94-95
   non-financial, 137-38, 141-42
   psychology of, 216
   techniques of, 98-99
   of underachievers, 99-100

N

Names, remembering, 101
Natural breaks, 204
Needs Analysis, 146-47

O

Objectives:
   appraisals tied to, 132-33
   routine, defining, 176-77, 179
   statement of, 153-54
   See also Goals
Odiorne, George, 19, 150
On Medical Education (Huxley), 62
Organization Development, 86-89
   key policies for, 86-87
   needs and, 89
   process of, 87
   profiling, 152

P

Passing the buck, 210
Performance:
   appraisal of, 122-29, 131-32, 135-36
   competence and, 90
   evaluation of, 91-92
   marginal, causes of, 133-35
   poor, reasons for, 196
   principles for improving, 216-17
   problems and, 90-91
Performance-based management (PBM), 148-51
   auditing of, 170-71
   basics of, 155
   benefits from, 149-50
   calendar events in, 169-70
   Chief Executive and, 150-51
   conditions for success in, 149
   cycle of, 160-64
   employee advantages of, 165
   goal-setting in, 180-81
   guides to implementing, 151-52
   inertia fought by, 169
   lack of enthusiasm for, 166-67
   methods for success in, 165-66
   organization benefits of, 160
   precautions for implementation of, 168
   profile for, 152-53
   reasons for failure of, 167
   stages of, 159
Personal development goals, 68-70

U

Underachievers, motivation of, 99-100
United States Chamber of Commerce, 96

V

Visitors, 200-201

W

Work ethic, 92-93
Written communications, 207-8